Texas Crime Stories

Texas Crime Stories

Volume I

Riding Herd on the Lawless

Robert Riggs

Dedication

"To the victims whose voices deserve to be heard."

My wife, Elizabeth, the steadfast 'keeper of the flame' who holds our family together, and my beloved children, Patrick and Katie Lee, and my sister Sherry have provided unwavering support, sustaining me through both triumphs and trials."

They endured countless late nights, missed celebrations, and anxious moments as I doggedly pursued stories—both near home and abroad—amid bullets, threats, and uncertainty.

I owe the disciplined pursuit of truth to my late father, Stanley Riggs, and my late uncle and namesake, Robert Sims—humble men shaped by Depression-era hardship who served our nation in World War II with honor and distinction.

My father's camaraderie with law enforcement in Paris, Texas—FBI Agent Del Drake, Texas Ranger Max Womack, State Troopers, and local officers—instilled in me an early respect for justice and truth.

I was fortunate to learn under remarkable mentors—particularly professors Alan Stacell and Rodney Hill at Texas A&M's College of Architecture, whose creative insights have enriched my storytelling. On Capitol Hill, the late Baron Shacklette, administrative assistant to Rep. Wright Patman, refined my investigative instincts, while Bob Schieffer of CBS News and the late Bob Squier helped open the door to broadcast journalism. Marty Haag and John Miller at WFAA-TV stood steadfastly by me, believing in my work through pivotal moments.

On the crime beat, I forged enduring friendships with true icons of justice, courage, and professionalism. If tragedy ever touched my family, these are the investigators I would want on the case: John Moriarty, Bill Johnston, Deputy U.S. Marshal Mike McNamara, Sheriff Parnell McNamara, Louis Fawcett, Tase Bailey, and Tim Steglich—each relentless in their pursuit of wrongdoing.

The first season of True Crime Reporter® uncovered the troubling release of serial killer Kenneth McDuff, resulting in our acclaimed streaming TV documentary, "Freed To Kill." Special gratitude goes to Executive Producers Seth Isler and Susan Sullivan, whose vision brought this critical story vividly to life.

The Texas Prison Museum, located in Huntsville, Texas, and its Director David Stacks continue to assist with my storytelling on the True Crime Reporter® podcast.

One day, my grandchildren will fully understand not only my experiences in war but also my journey through the shadowed corridors of the Texas prison system and the pursuit of truth in a complex world.

In closing, I share the timeless wisdom inscribed on my late father's business card—words that reflect the essence of my life's journey:

In my chain of friendships
There are many individual links
Some are steel, some silver and some gold
But nothing to me in life is more
Sacred than the friendship
Of a good friend.

Table of Contents

Texas Crime Stories

Preface

For more than four decades, I have walked a narrow and often treacherous path that winds from crime scenes to courtrooms and prison cellblocks. My journey as an investigative reporter has taken me from the invasion of Iraq as an embedded reporter under fire to the solemn halls of Congress and The White House and deep into the darkest recesses of criminal minds in Texas.

The stories you are about to read in "Texas Crime Stories Volume I: Riding Herd On The Lawless" are not merely true crime accounts—they are chronicles ripped directly from my reporter's notebook, steeped in authenticity and enriched by decades of exclusive access and trust earned through the relentless pursuit of the truth. These narratives span notorious serial killers, malevolent killers, audacious fugitives, and cunning con artists, each story meticulously reported and vividly told.

In launching my podcast, True Crime Reporter®, I sought not merely to entertain but to inform, educate, and, above all, humanize stories often lost in sensationalism. The podcast became my platform to leverage decades of investigative journalism into conversations that matter, allowing listeners an unprecedented look into criminal cases through exclusive interviews with law enforcement, survivors, and, on occasion, even the criminals themselves.

My investigative work also led to the creation of the acclaimed streaming television documentary, "Freed To Kill," which revealed the unsettling truth behind the release of serial killer Kenneth McDuff under a cloud of corruption. The documentary underscored systemic failures within the criminal justice system and profoundly resonated with audiences both domestically and internationally, further solidifying my commitment to accountability and reform.

The roots of my investigative passion were formed early, shaped by a Texas heritage rich with stories of justice, frontier law, and unwavering courage. My education in architecture and construction at Texas A&M University might seem an unlikely foundation for a career in journalism. Still, it taught me precision, structure, and the art of building stories piece by meticulous piece.

Throughout my career, I have received honors, notably a Peabody Award for investigative reporting—yet it is the quiet moments, the whispered confessions, the look in a victim's eyes, and the pursuit of elusive truths that have defined my work. Whether standing before audiences at live events, crafting television documentaries, or narrating these stories for print and audio, my purpose remains the same: to shed light into darkness and offer clarity in chaos.

With "Texas Crime Stories Volume I," I invite you to journey with me through the winding trails of Texas justice, where the truth is often stranger—and far more compelling—than fiction. As we ride herd on the lawless together, my hope is not only to intrigue you but to remind you that at the heart of every crime story lies a lesson in humanity, resilience, and sometimes, redemption.

Robert Riggs
Investigative Reporter

Introduction

Texas is more than a state—it is a land of legends and contradictions, where sweeping plains meet bustling metropolises and frontier myths brush against modern realities. It is where rugged individualism is celebrated, yet within its vast borders lie darker narratives that unsettle even the toughest among us.

In "Texas Crime Stories: Riding Herd On The Lawless," I invite you into a world hidden beneath the bold image of cowboy boots and oil rigs, into shadowy corners where crime often writes a more compelling—and disturbing—story. As an investigative reporter who has spent decades traversing crime scenes, courtrooms, and penitentiary corridors, I've witnessed firsthand the raw impact of violence, greed, and desperation etched into the Lone Star State's history.

From the chilling corridors of Texas Death Row, where inmates like Richard Tabler ignited political firestorms from smuggled cell phones, to the heart-wrenching saga of Annie Laurie Williams, whose gruesome murder of her sons shocked the nation, these stories peel away layers of humanity's darkest impulses.

You'll follow the audacious escapes of Dennis Wayne Hope and Martin Gurule, whose cunning and desperation tested the might of Texas prison security, and delve into the bizarre saga of Charles J. Woods, a bank robber and fugitive whose mysterious disappearance intersects with CIA conspiracies and drug smuggling in Mena, Arkansas. Experience the haunting echoes of the 1974 siege at Huntsville's "Walls Unit," where Fred Gomez Carrasco, a notorious drug lord, orchestrated the longest prison siege in American history.

Explore the surreal violence of Doug Feldman, a mass killer whose calculated shootings terrorized Dallas highways, and uncover the dark charm of Sandra Bridewell, known infamously as "The Black Widow" of Dallas high society, whose sinister narrative intertwines wealth, deception, and death.

These narratives are not simply about crime; they illuminate the profound struggles between good and evil, justice and impunity, and order and chaos. They honor the resilience of victims, the courage of law enforcement, and the tireless quest for truth by those who refuse to turn away.

This anthology offers no escape from reality but rather a deeper, more troubling understanding of it. For those brave enough to ride alongside, welcome to the real Texas—unvarnished, unforgettable, and undeniably compelling.

The Bible Thumping Dark Angel

A Tragic Easter Morning

In the quiet resplendence of an Easter Sunday morning, the young, charismatic pastor approached the pulpit at the Crossroads Baptist Church with a heavy heart.

Just days after the tragic and untimely loss of his wife to suicide, Matt Baker stood before his congregation, appearing not just as a shepherd to his flock but as a testament to the human spirit's resilience in the face of unspeakable grief.

"Just like Jesus," Baker told his congregation that his 31-year-old wife Kari had made a "triumphal entry" into heaven. "Death could not control her," he said. "Death could not control her at all."

Kari Baker had taken an overdose following the anniversary of the death of her child seven years earlier to brain cancer.

As Matt Baker spoke, the air within the sanctuary thickened with emotion, a silent, collective embrace for a man who, in his moment of profound personal despair, chose to stand before them with messages of hope and renewal.

The pews were filled with individuals moved not only by the depth of his grief but by the strength and vulnerability he displayed in sharing his pain so openly.

The Congregation's Admiration

The seventy-five-member congregation idolized the 35-year-old, five-foot-seven pastor.

On any given Sunday, many people felt Baker preached sermons directly to them. He emoted a big personality coupled with a firm handshake. He greeted congregants with sentences peppered with "God loves you."

Baker was boyish-looking, blue-eyed, with a round face, full cheeks, and a broad forehead topped by a dark brown burr haircut.

His small church, located in Lorena, a small community on the south side of Waco, Texas, sat in the orbit of Baylor University—the largest Baptist university in the world–at the center of Baptist theology.

Baker met his wife there 12 years earlier when he was a senior majoring in church recreation.

The Foundations of Faith

At six years old, Baker had answered the call that traditionally follows a Baptist church service. He walked down the aisle to publicly surrender his life to Christ.

He faithfully attended Sunday school, sang in youth choirs, went on mission trips, and on a high school retreat, announced he would dedicate his life to the Baptist ministry.

His classmates described him as a phenomenal Christian young man.

Baker met Kari at First Baptist Church in Waco. She was smitten by him, and they married three months later.

Kari became the quintessential preacher's wife, with a sunny spirit that would brighten a room. Her fresh Meg Ryan look resembled the movie Sleepless in Seattle.

Blonde bangs in a pixie-style cut hairstyle caressed the top of her thin eyebrows above beaming crystal-blue eyes.

She led Bible study groups and kept an open door as the couple moved from church to church.

But there were dark secrets about Matt Baker's sexual proclivities.

Leaders of the Southern Baptist Convention, America's largest Protestant denomination, had covered up reports of sexual abuse by its ministers for years.

The Bakers appeared to be the portrait of a happy, wholesome Baptist family.

The Baker Family Tragedy

In late 1998, doctors discovered a brain tumor in one-year-old Kassidy. Following surgery, the toddler spent three months recovering in the hospital.

But her recovery was short-lived. In the early morning hours of March 22, 1999, Matt Baker found their daughter lifeless in her crib at home – she had stopped breathing.

When a child precedes a parent in death, it's a hard thing to come to terms with.

The distraught mother cradled Kassidy's body in her arms and gently rocked her after she had been pronounced dead at the hospital.

15

At the visitation before the funeral, Kari hugged her daughter's casket and wept a river of tears.

She returned to the children's section of Waco's Oakwood Cemetery and dug at the freshly turned dirt on her daughter's grave with her bare hands as if she were trying to reach her.

Grief-stricken, Kari took to her bed and would not get up. Members of the William Creek Baptist church brought food and flowers. They built an outdoor prayer garden where Kari often stood and sobbed into her hands.

Matt Baker claimed Kari ran out of the house wielding a knife once, threatening to end things until he rescued her. They cried together, he said.

After a series of moves to other churches, the family returned to Waco to be close to Kari's parents and Kassidy's grave.

Kari taught the third grade and entertained students at lunch by skipping around the room.

The Bakers brought a third daughter into the world named Grace.

Suspicions About Matt Baker

But beneath her happy facade, Kari confided suspicions that Matt Baker was having an affair and planning to kill her.

She told her therapist that she had found a small, unlabeled bottle of pills in his briefcase.

Kari's Final Days

On April 7, 2006, Matt Baker, his wife Kari, and daughters Kensi and Grace were seen late that afternoon at the YMCA.

They watched their oldest daughter, Kensi, at swim practice.

Kari seemed upbeat, cheerfully greeting the people she knew.

It was the last time Kari Baker would be seen alive in public.

The Night of Kari's Death

A few minutes after midnight, Matt Baker made an emergency phone call. He told a 911 operator, "I think my wife just committed suicide."

Paramedics arrived in less than five minutes. They found Kari's body on the bedroom floor by the bed, her lips blue.

A bottle of Unisom, a nonprescription sleeping medication, with only two pills left in the 32-pill bottle, rested on the bedside table.

They also found a typed suicide note written to Matt. "Please continue to be the great Dad to our little girls," it read. "Love them every day for me. I am sorry. I love you. Kari."

Baker told police officers from the small town of Hewitt, where they lived, that Kari had been talking about suicide for the past two weeks.

But said he didn't take her seriously.

Baker told police that Kari had vomited in the bathroom after arriving home from the YMCA.

He said she got into bed, drank a couple of wine coolers, and asked him to rent the movie *When A Man Loves A Woman*, which they had seen on their first date. Baker said he tucked his girls into bed and left home around 11:15 PM. He claimed to have stopped at a gas station, picked up the movie at a video store, and got home shortly after midnight.

He found the bedroom door locked and used a screwdriver to open it. That's when Baker says he found that his wife was not breathing, just like he had found their daughter Kassidy.

He tried CPR to no avail. Fluid spurted out of her mouth and covered her face and hair, he said.

A Questionable Investigation

The detective from the small-town police department took pity on the popular young preacher.

Under Texas law, he was supposed to call a Justice of the Peace known as a JP to the scene for a formal ruling about the death.

Instead, he read the suicide note over the phone to the JP. They concluded it was suicide and that an autopsy would not be necessary.

Kari Baker's death certificate stated, "Overdose of Unisom Sleep-Aid."

A Relentless Former Prosecutor Investigates

Former federal prosecutor Bill Johnston conducted an independent investigation many months later at the request of Kari Baker's mother, Linda.

Johnston was shocked by the lack of evidence: "The police work was dreadful, and the photos were dreadful. They took two or three photos. It turns out that the sergeant who was in charge of the so-called investigation was afraid of bodies, and he didn't really want to get too close to Kari's corpse.

Johnston says there was sparse evidence for his investigation to work with.

"They took a photograph of the note and a couple of photographs of the pill bottle," recalled Johnston with deep contempt in his voice. Johnston and two retired law enforcement investigators who were assisting him immediately thought the scene of the purported suicide looked staged, "It was one of the first things that we noticed; the bedside scene looked a little like the one for actress Marilyn Monroe. There was a 50-count bottle of sleeping pills with two tablets left. It was made to look as if she had 48 tablets of a generic brand of sleeping pills.

The typed suicide note also aroused Johnston's suspicion, "I'd never seen a typed suicide note. That was weird. Never heard of it. The note was unsigned, so there was nothing attributable to Kari in handwriting or otherwise."

At the end of Kari Baker's funeral service, Matt Baker stoically stood by the pulpit with his daughters beside him. He hugged the faithful, who lined up to offer their condolences.

Baker pledged that he would be back at Crossroads Baptist Church the next Sunday—Easter Sunday—to preach the glory of the empty tomb. "God has not abandoned me," he whispered to one friend. "He will give me the strength to carry on."

A Mother's Pursuit of Truth

A week after Matt Baker's emotional Easter sermon, Kari Baker's three aunts and a cousin expressed their suspicions to her mother, Linda Dulin.

All of them had heard stories about Matt Baker's sexual indiscretions. They revealed that a teenage girl they all knew had come to see little Kassidy at the hospital back in 1998.

The teenager said Baker pulled her aside, put his hand on her leg, and asked her to go to an empty visitors' room with him.

Another sister revealed that Baker hugged her teenage daughter, brushed his hand against her breast, and questioned if she was wearing panties.

Then, they revealed a startling truth. Kari had confided to her therapist that she thought her husband was planning to kill her.

Taking a chapter out of *Dateline*, they tried to investigate but got nowhere with amateur sleuthing.

Kari's mother asked the Chief of the Hewitt Police Department to reopen the investigation. She said the Chief told her there was no evidence and she was wasting her time.

That's when she went home and called Bill Johnston.

Uncovering Matt Baker's Dark Secrets

"When Kari Baker's mom, Linda, came to us with the case, she said, 'I guess my daughter killed herself. But I hate to think that, and my sisters think his guy [Baker] is not right and may have done something to her. I don't know if it's worse to have your daughter murder or to have killed herself," recalled Johnston.

Johnston assembled a team of seasoned investigators and reached out to Tom Bevel, a renowned blood splatter analyst based in Oklahoma. As Johnston began describing the suicide scene, Bevel cut him off abruptly to ask, "Was Matt Baker having an affair?"

The question gave Johnston pause. Bevel explained that, in his experience, when a preacher is caught in an affair, his career—and his life as he knows it—could be destroyed. But if the preacher's wife dies, whether by murder or apparent suicide, he often transforms into a figure of sympathy: the grieving widower. The implications for the case were profound.

Bill Johnston had built his career as a relentless federal prosecutor with a reputation for pursuing the truth at any cost. Standing six-foot-four, with dark, thick black hair and piercing eyes, Johnston's presence alone could unsettle criminals. He often wore an oversized western belt buckle, a relic from his days riding bucking broncos at Texas A&M University—a symbol of his grit and resilience. He knew how to get knocked down and climb right back on. Johnston was fearless and took on cases that others shied away from, deeming them too difficult to win.

L-R U.S. Deputy U.S. Marshal Mike McNamara, U.S. Prosecutor Bill Johnston, Deputy U.S. Marshal Parnell McNamara on the manhunt of serial killer Keneth McDuff. 1992

Fourteen years earlier, Johnston had spearheaded the manhunt for serial killer Kenneth McDuff. At the time, other agencies had declined to investigate the disappearance of a convenience store clerk in Waco, Texas, claiming there was no probable cause. Undeterred, Johnston, along with Deputy U.S. Marshals Mike McNamara and his brother Parnell, launched a nationwide manhunt. Their investigation ultimately led to the downfall of the Texas Parole Board chairman, who had been accused of selling paroles to violent criminals, including killers.

Johnston had law enforcement in his blood. His late father had been a Dallas prosecutor involved in the Jack Ruby case, the man who killed presidential assassin Lee Harvey Oswald. As for Johnston, he had never lost a jury trial in the Federal Courthouse in Waco.

For the Kari Baker investigation, Johnston recruited retired U.S. Marshal Mike McNamara, a legend in Central Texas law enforcement. Lean and steely-eyed, McNamara, with his gray hair, white Stetson, and cowboy boots, was the embodiment of the Old West—a modern-day Wyatt Earp. Known for being heavily armed, he had dedicated his life to upholding the law.

The Evidence Mounts

One lead suggested that Matt Baker had made inappropriate advances toward a 14-year-old girl when he was a student counselor at Baylor University. McNamara, never one to back down from confrontation, cornered an assistant preacher about the allegations. When pressed on why Baker hadn't been fired, the preacher brushed it off, saying, "Well, he has a calling. He's going to the seminary, and we don't want to interfere with that. If the Lord called him, we don't want to stand in the way."

As the investigation deepened, a Waco detective tipped Johnston off, suggesting he look into the police department's records on Baker. In 1997, a female athletic trainer had filed a complaint against Baker for attempted sexual assault, which she said occurred in the locker room at Baylor's Floyd Casey Stadium six years earlier.

Johnston obtained the police report through the Texas Open Records Act, but the victim's name had been redacted. Holding the document up to the light, he revealed the obscured name. His investigator, John Bennett, a former undercover agent with the Texas Department of Public Safety, tracked the woman down in West Texas. She explained that when she had attempted to press charges, the police turned her away because the statute of limitations had expired.

"There were so many opportunities for someone to do the right thing regarding Matt Baker," Johnston said, his frustration palpable. "But no one did because they didn't want to tarnish their image."

According to the police report, the woman first met Matt Baker while she was a student and he was an athletic trainer at Baylor University. One day, Baker turned off the lights in the locker room and trapped her, attempting to assault her sexually. She broke free from his grip and immediately reported the incident to the head athletic trainer. He assured her the matter had been reported to the Waco Police Department.

Traumatized and struggling with the psychological aftermath, the woman left Baylor. Years later, still seeking justice, she was horrified to discover that Baker had faced no consequences for the assault. Instead, he kept his position and was eventually promoted to a leadership role at the First Baptist Church in Waco.

As Johnston dug deeper into the case, his investigation uncovered a disturbing pattern: Baker had a history of predatory behavior, with multiple accounts pointing to him as a serial sexual predator. However, despite the mounting evidence of his misconduct, Johnston had yet to find concrete proof linking Baker to the murder of his wife.

Breaking Down an Alibi

Johnston began systematically dismantling Matt Baker's alibi for the night of his wife's alleged suicide. Baker claimed that Kari had asked him to fill the car with gas for errands she planned to run the next day and to pick up a movie from the video store. He even produced gasoline receipts to corroborate his story. But there was one glaring problem—during the 911 call, Baker told first responders that Kari's lips were blue and her body felt cold to the touch.

This is where Baker's alibi crumbled. Johnston pointed out that Kari Baker had been dead much longer than it took for Matt Baker to run those so-called errands. "She had double lividity," Johnston noted, referring to the telltale purple discoloration on both sides of Kari's body, caused by the pooling of blood after death. This indicated her body had been moved at least twice and that she had been dead for hours before Matt Baker dialed for help.

Without an autopsy performed at the time of her death, Johnston knew he needed experts to examine Kari's body for any remaining traces of sleeping pills or other drugs that could have been used to mask the truth.

At this point, Johnston enlisted the help of a Texas Ranger, someone he had worked hard to get involved in the case. Johnson grew more frustrated when the Hewitt police wanted no part of it—they considered the case closed, labeling it a suicide. "They knew reopening it would embarrass them, but they stuck to their conclusion: suicide and poor preacher, right?"

With the Texas Ranger's assistance, Johnston obtained a court order to exhume Kari Baker's body. Exhumation autopsies are never as thorough or revealing as initial ones, but investigators still hoped for answers.

The autopsy uncovered some significant findings. Although post-exhumation tests aren't always conclusive, the toxicology report revealed traces of sleeping aid Ambien in her muscle tissue.

However, the report couldn't determine the exact amount or strength, as exhumed bodies don't provide the same level of clarity. Still, the discovery of Ambien raised immediate questions. "We checked with everyone close to her—her mother, her aunts—anyone who might know if she had a prescription. No one had ever known her to take Ambien, said Johnston.

This opened another avenue of investigation into Baker's computer.

Computer Forensics

Johnston was eager to find out if Matt Baker had searched online for information about sleeping pills. Still, Baker had conveniently discarded his computer, claiming it was incompatible with a new printer.

Undeterred, Johnston and his team turned their attention to Baker's other place of employment. In addition to his role as a preacher, Baker worked as a chaplain at the Waco Center for Youth, a facility for children who needed guidance—some orphans, others troubled, all vulnerable. It seemed like an ideal setting for someone in a position of trust to sexually abuse children. It raised a red flag. "I've seen enough sexual predator cases to know this is exactly the kind of environment predators target for vulnerable young women," Johnston remarked.

Recognizing the gravity of the situation, Johnston dispatched Mike McNamara, the retired U.S. Marshal known for his unflinching sense of duty. The challenge was that, without an official law enforcement investigation, Johnston and his team were conducting a private inquiry, gathering evidence the best they could and hoping to pass it along to the authorities.

"We were privately prosecuting, so to speak," Johnston explained. "There was no official investigation ahead of us. We were working with almost nothing and did not have subpoena power to compel people to talk to us."

When McNamara went to the Waco Center for Youth, where Matt Baker worked as a chaplain, he uncovered several peculiar and helpful details. First, he spoke with Baker's secretary, who mentioned something odd. "Oh, Matt? Yeah, he didn't really leave his office much," she said. McNamara was taken aback. If Baker was supposed to be a chaplain, when was he ministering to the youth? Leading Bible studies or counseling? "I don't recall him doing any group counseling or much of anything with the kids," the secretary added.

McNamara then spoke to the IT administrator, who revealed something strange. He pointed McNamara toward a woman who had witnessed something unusual on a state holiday shortly after Kari Baker's death. She reported seeing Matt Baker leave the Waco Center for Youth that day, carrying something large and heavy, wrapped up, and placing it in the trunk of his car. It was an eerie sight, especially since the center was nearly empty that day.

But there was more. The IT guy explained, "Something odd happened with the computers that same day." He told McNamara that Baker must have thought he was clever by focusing on his computer tower but overlooked the center's server. On the holiday, the IT logs showed Baker's computer going offline, along with his secretary's, within minutes of each other. When they came back online, the configuration was different.

It turned out that Baker had swapped his computer with his secretary's. He had peeled off the stickers from his tower and placed them on hers, then took her computer—now disguised as his. When the secretary returned the next day, she noticed her computer was missing, but in reality, it was Baker's machine that had been taken.

Baker's plan might have worked if it weren't for the server logs. The logs revealed that Baker spent most of his time online searching for pornography. But late one evening, as Johnston and McNamara sifted through files on a disc from Baker's computer, something unusual caught their eye. Ambien, a sleeping pill prescribed for insomnia flashed on the screen. The file appeared in a scrambled mess of data, so Johnston sent it to Noel Kersh, a forensic computer expert in Houston, Texas, for analysis.

A few days later, Kersh got back to Johnston with a breakthrough. He confirmed that Baker had visited an offshore pharmacy and placed an order for Ambien. From what he could gather, Baker had successfully ordered the drug in the weeks leading up to Kari's death. Now we had something substantial to support our theory.

Johnston now had evidence to support his murder theory. He believed that Baker had crushed up Ambien and slipped it into a drink Kari had asked for—a specific type of wine cooler. His theory was that the drug made her drowsy, perhaps even unconscious and that Baker then smothered her with a pillow to finish the job.

The few photos taken by police of the bedroom scene showed large, heavy pillows that were heavy enough to suffocate someone. Now, with the Ambien order confirmed, the pieces were starting to fall into place. This also explained why Baker had gone to such lengths to switch out his computer—he was trying to cover his tracks.

Unfortunately, crucial evidence had already been lost. The wine cooler, which could have provided forensic proof of the Ambien, had long since been discarded. Johnston needed to figure out how the drug might have been used. "We conducted an experiment: one of our colleagues had a prescription for Ambien, so we invited him to the office. We replicated the scenario, ordering the same wine coolers and crushing a few Ambien pills into one of them. Our colleague tasted all the wine coolers and couldn't distinguish the one spiked with Ambien from the others. It was clear that Kari wouldn't have been able to tell either."

If the pillows had been collected as forensic evidence, it could have detected that material was in Kari's nasal passages or lungs. Frustrated, Johnston said, "It was too late. If an autopsy had been performed shortly after her death, we might have detected signs of suffocation—particularly in the eyes, where blood vessels expand and burst when someone is strangled or suffocated. It's a telltale sign. But by the time we exhumed her body, those clues were long gone."

Johnston's Fishing Expedition

"At this stage of his investigation, Johnston had exhausted all possible avenues to gather evidence. So, Johnston sued Baker for wrongful death under Texas civil law. "To my surprise—and likely due to his arrogance and misplaced confidence—Baker allowed me to take his deposition under oath. I limited my questions because I didn't have enough information.

I let him describe the purported suicide scene, hoping to get a basic account on record. But the session got cut short, and that gave me the chance to request another one."

During the second deposition, Johnston went on a "fishing expedition." He searched for evidence to discover incriminating details by exploring all available avenues, hoping that something relevant or valuable would emerge.

"My approach was strategic. I took a sympathetic tone: 'Poor Matt, you poor fella. Let's just clear a few things up and put this behind us. It was all calculated. I wanted him comfortable enough to talk freely, so I let him walk me through the crime scene again."

Johnston asked meticulous questions to lock down every detail, every timeline. His goal was to solidify Baker's version of events—so there would be no room for him to change his story later. "He described being away from the house for about 15 to 18 minutes. I suspected that he might eventually claim she had already taken the pills before he left, so I carefully laid a trap."

In anticipation of Baker's defense strategy, Johnston pressed, "Your daughters were in the house at the time, correct?' And he said, Oh, yes. Then I said, And you're a good father—you wouldn't leave your girls without proper adult supervision, right? He agreed, of course. So I pressed further if Kari had been in any way incapacitated, you would have made sure someone capable was there to take care of the girls, wouldn't you?' Again, he agreed. Then I asked the key question: 'So, Kari was perfectly fine when you left?' He confirmed she was."

"By doing that, I locked him into his timeline. He couldn't later claim that she was already under the influence of the pills before he left. The story was set, and now, so was his alibi."

Baker's timeline undermined his alibi. By his admission, he was not gone long enough for her to die. The lividity found on her body indicated Kari had been dead for at least two hours before Baker called 911.

Led Down the Primrose Path

Johnston, a skilled interrogator, skillfully led Matt Baker down the primrose path, and he had one more card to play.

When the media scrutiny increased, Matt Baker moved out of Central Texas to live with his parents in the Hill Country outside of Austin. Johnston's investigators received a call from a hair stylist who recognized a front cover photograph of Baker in a *Texas Monthly* Story. She divulged that after an appointment, Baker went home with her, where they had consensual sexual relations. She told the investigator that she would never have let Baker into her home if she had known who he was.

Texas Monthly's circulation extended far beyond Texas, reaching readers in New York, California, and nationwide. It provided more bait for Johnston's fishing expedition.

"The cover had him holding a cross and a Bible, looking pitiful. And right above his photo were the words: 'Did this Baptist preacher murder his wife?' That was the question looming over him. So when I deposed him, I couldn't resist going there."

Johnston began deliberately, leading Baker down the primrose path with a carefully crafted series of questions. Baker, solemnly nodding, confirmed the tragic losses of both his wife and daughters, playing the part of the grieving widower.

Baker acknowledged the tragedy, insisting he remained loyal to his late wife.

Johnston "set the hook," which refers to the moment when a fisherman pulls sharply on the line to ensure that the hook firmly catches in the fish's mouth, preventing it from slipping away. In this context, Johnston had guided the Baker into a carefully constructed trap to catch him in his own words.

In a sympathetic tone, Johnston asked, "And since you're grieving, I bet you haven't married anyone else, have you, Matt? I bet you haven't even been with anyone else since your wife passed, right?"

Baker took the bait and professed that he could not bring himself to have a sexual relationship with anyone else. With the hook firmly in place, Johnston leaned in and asked, "Matt, since moving down here to the Hill Country, do you get your hair cut?" Johnston asked, watching Baker's face flush red, and his voice grew noticeably nervous. Johnston dropped the bomb, "Well, did you ever have a female barber? And did you ever go to her house after a haircut?"

Baker fumbled, stammering that he didn't know or couldn't recall. Sensing his discomfort, Johnston pressed harder. "You did. You went to her house, and one thing led to another, didn't it?" Baker tried to feign ignorance muttering that he didn't know what Johnston was talking about.

Johnston wasn't about to back off. "You two had sex, didn't you? Not that there's anything wrong with that, Matt, but you did, didn't you?"

By now, Baker was visibly flustered, red-faced, and cornered. Johnston chuckles now as he recalls that Baker finally blurted out, "Well, I, uh, 'gratifacated her', or some similar nonsense, grasping for words."

Baker apparently could not bring himself to say "fornicated." Johnston admits that Baker's sexual dalliance with the hair stylist had nothing to do with the case, "I just couldn't leave it alone. His hypocrisy was so bitter in my mouth that I thought, I've got to ask."

The Discovery of Baker's Mistress

Johnston had taken his private investigation as far as it could go. "We had gathered evidence suspicions, and we believed we had identified a girlfriend. She was the daughter of a music minister, and while we had some proof of an affair, when we talked to her, her story didn't add up. She denied everything, but her answers left us unconvinced. By the end, we had a 'silver platter' of evidence to hand off to Texas Ranger Matt Cawthon and the McLennan County District Attorney, which is exactly what we did."

The District Attorney subpoenaed Baker's mistress, 27-year-old Vanessa Bulls, to testify before the grand jury. At first, Bulls wanted to plead the Fifth Amendment, refusing to incriminate herself. But once the District Attorney granted her immunity, she had no choice but to speak.

Johnston says that she revealed a story to the grand jury that was one of the most horrifying accounts ever told at trial. "Many people later questioned why the DA granted immunity when she wasn't directly involved in the murder but knew so much afterward—and even stayed with Baker for a time."

Bulls' testified that Baker confessed that he had murdered his wife. The account confirmed Johnston's theory of how Baker committed the homicide. "He explained in chilling detail that he first drugged Kari to make her sleepy, then smothered her with a pillow. According to him, after he thought she was dead, he removed the pillow and looked at his handiwork. But then Kari gasped for air, struggling to breathe. So he pressed the pillow back down and suffocated her until the job was done. She had tried to come back to life, and he finished her off. This wasn't speculation—this was what he confessed to her, and she shared that grim story with the jury."

"It didn't end there. Bull's testimony, combined with the other evidence gathered by Johnston's investigation, including the woman who Baker had tried to rape her years earlier in the Baylor locker room, painted a chilling picture.

"We also uncovered a pattern: Baker had been quietly moved from one church to another whenever he 'acted weird' or when something concerning happened. No one held him accountable—they just passed the problem along," concluded Johnston.

Bulls testified that Baker confessed to killing his wife so they could be together. Johnston says there was another more sinister motive, "he saw himself as a 'dark angel,' deciding who lives and dies. We also found out that the day after Kari's death—whether by murder, as we believe, or suicide, as he claimed—Baker had erased her completely. The magnets and family photos on the refrigerator were gone, and pictures of the new 'mommy,' the girlfriend, had already replaced them. It was as if Kari had never existed, wiped from his life."

Johnston says Baker quickly positioned his girlfriend as the new mother for his children without a second thought. "That level of detachment, that ability to just erase someone like that—it shows what we were dealing with a cold, calculating, and selfish individual. A psychopath, perhaps a sociopath. Would he kill again? I have no doubt he would."

Johnston suspects that Baker may have also murdered his one-year-old daughter, Kassidy, who was home recovering from brain tumor surgery. "She was very ill and she was on oxygen. She died in her crib. The circumstances of that are bizarre." Johnston says Baker got up from bed to check on his daughter in the middle of the night and said he found her dead. Later, at the hospital, a physician stumbled upon Baker tampering with Kassidy's breathing tube to place it back in the correct position.

The Dark Angel

"Our investigator called Baker a "Dark Angel," that he decides who lives and dies, and it needs to suit him. So, milking sympathy for the little girl had already happened. And she was an expensive distraction to his life. And we believe he murdered her. We believe he murdered her in her crib. This guy was a cold-blooded killer who represented himself to the rest of the world as a saintly man, who posed for the cover of *Texas Monthly Magazine*, holding his cross and prayerfully looking at the camera. He was the ultimate hypocrite. He was a killer. A sorry, sorry, human. He's rotting in prison right now in Texas. Thank God. Literally, thank God."

The Trial of Matt Baker

When Matt Baker's murder trial opened in Waco, people eager to hear the prosecution's star witness, Vanessa Bulls packed the courtroom. the gallery was packed.

Baker's mistress had struck an immunity deal with the prosecution in exchange for her testimony.

She bore an uncanny resemblance to Kari Baker in her younger days.

Baker's dyed blonde hair, styled straight, cascaded over her shoulders, framing her oval face. Eye shadow accentuated her dark eyes, and mascara coated her eyelashes.

She did not exude a girl-next-door look or sexiness. She wore pants on wide hips topped with a grey blouse with a subtle, darker grey pattern, with an understated appearance. The blouse featured a button-up front, complemented by a layered, ruffled design around her neckline.

This was the moment everybody anxiously awaited.

Bulls, a middle school teacher, testified in gripping detail about her four-month-long affair with Baker.

She told the jury, "I am sitting here because a manipulative liar wearing the mask of God came into my life, and I am here to put him where he needs to be."

Bulls, whose father was a music minister, said she met Matt Baker in September 2005, when she started attending Crossroads Baptist Church, where Baker was pastor.

A few months later, she said, Baker spotted her sitting alone in the sanctuary before the service started and asked about her divorce.

He told her that whoever found her was going to be a lucky man, Bulls said, adding that his flirtations grew more obvious as the months wore on.

"One time, he heard me talking about dating, and he said: 'Oh, don't date other guys. Just date your pastor,'" Bulls recalled.

Baker revealed he had gotten a vasectomy and was free from sexual diseases she said. She added he admitted to cheating on Kari Baker a few times, calling her "clueless."

Baker started counseling Bulls after her divorce. Their relationship grew into an affair beginning in March 2006, a month before Baker murdered his wife.

A Cold-Blooded Killer

Bulls said Baker wanted Kari out of his life and could not divorce her because it would kill his career.

Baker discussed killing Kari by "tampering with the brakes on her car, a drive-by shooting, and hanging her and making it look like a suicide," she said.

He decided to make his wife's death appear to be an overdose of sleeping pills.

As their two children slept down the hall, Baker gave his wife doctored pills, handcuffed her to the bed, and kissed her until she fell asleep. He kissed her on the forehead and told her to hug or kiss Kassidy for him, Bulls said.

Baker then smothered her with a pillow, typed a suicide note on the bedroom computer, and placed his wife's hands on the note to put her fingerprints on it, Bulls said.

Baker later locked the door to the bedroom, left his two daughters sleeping down the hall, and went to rent a movie and gas up the car, she said. He came home about 45 minutes later and called 9-1-1.

Even though she was aware of the murder plot, Bulls never voluntarily came forward.

She and her family went to Baker's house hours after Kari's death to pay their respects. Baker winked at her, she said.

Five days later, she went back to the Baker home, and Baker recounted how he killed his wife.

She told the jury that Baker said he would tell her once and never wanted to speak of the murder again.

"He said: 'You know you are stuck with me, right? Because you know about it and are just as guilty as I am?' He said God is a forgiving God, and he has forgiven him."

Bulls said Baker later threatened her. He sent her the lyrics to a song titled "Dirty Little Secret emphasizing, "I'll keep you my dirty little secret. Don't tell anyone or you'll be just another regret."

The Devil Can Cite Scripture

The jury deliberated more than six hours before finding former Baptist Minister Matt Baker guilty of drugging and suffocating his wife Kari to death.

During the punishment phase, when juries in Texas rule on sentencing, the court heard from a dozen women who took the stand to testify that Matt Baker had approached them sexually.

Matt Baker is serving a 65-year murder sentence in Texas maximum security Michael Unit.

He becomes eligible for parole in the year 2039 at age 67.

Prosecutor Crawford Long, who is well versed in the classics, said that, in the end, Matt Baker reminded us of the quote from

Shakespeare's *The Merchant of Venice:* "The Devil can cite Scripture for his purpose."

Robert Riggs

The Malevolent Mommy

The 1950s Dream and a Family's Nightmare

The 1950s were called the "Happy Days". The war was over. The economy was booming. The American Dream was in full swing with a baby boom.

An estimated one baby was born every second in 1957.

The Lone Ranger was a hit TV show. Little boys acted out their mythical western adventures on stick horses.

But the dream became a nightmare for two little brothers in Texas. Their murders came at the hands of their knife-wielding mother.

The gruesome crime shocked the nation.

This is the 57-year-long story about the mother who murdered her sons with malice.

A Smiling Confession

L.R. Child Slayer Annie Laurie Williams, Defense Attorneys James Piperi and Percy Foreman. 1955

33-year-old Annie Laurie Williams flashed a big smile for a newspaper photographer. In the frame, her famous criminal defense attorney, Percy Foreman of Houston, held her plea bargain agreement up to the camera. Williams had admitted to murdering her two little boys.

Williams' expression gave no hint of the gruesome crime she had committed in February of 1955 in Pasadena, Texas.

The prim and proper-looking dime-store clerk appeared to beam with joy.

Williams wore a modest sweater buttoned to her neck. Her short banged, auburn hairstyle resembled the pixie cut that Audrey Hepburn debuted in the 1953 movie *Roman Holiday*.

The Crime's Impact on a Nation

Since her arrest on February 22, 1955, Mrs. Ann Williams had made front-page headlines across the country for the murders of her 8-year-old son Conrad and 9-year-old son Calvin.

Boldface type on the front page of Williams' hometown newspaper in Hammond, Indiana, screamed, "Mom Butchers 2 Sons."

The home edition of the Baytown Sun in Texas exclaimed, "Mother Admits Cutting Up Two Sons. Their Bikes Still There...Trailer Was Home To Dead Boys."

Baytown was home to one of the largest oil refineries in the world. Baytown and the neighboring community of Pasadena, where Williams lived, were located on the southeast side of Houston.

Newspapers featured photos of the boys with big grins on their faces dressed in striped shirts and solid color shorts, climbing on a jungle gym. Centered between them is a photo of their mom, Ann Williams, wearing horn-rimmed glasses, hands politely folded with a pensive expression on her face, looking like a librarian.

Introduction to a Dark Crime

So now. brace yourselves. We are about to get into the gory details of her murders provided by Louis Fawcett, a fugitive hunter for the Texas Department of Criminal Justice and member of an FBI Violent Crime Task Force in Dallas.

"Her boys, I think, were eight and nine years old. She told them they could go to the movies. She had an argument with her husband, who was in federal prison, somehow, I guess, through correspondence. She was upset and she told the boys they could go to a movie. Well, when they came home, she told him that they needed to take something for their cold and she gave him a big dose of cold medicine. They said we don't feel bad. But she insisted. She gave them an overdose and put them to sleep. Once she got them to sleep, she tied bandanas around their necks and tightened it up, and then drove the nail into the bandana into the head board of the bed to hold them there. When she was convinced that they were dead, she put their bodies in a bathtub full of lime and lye. She hoped to dissolve the body. And when that didn't work, she went to the store, bought a big sheet of plastic, and fabricated some bags. And she dismembered these boy's bodies completely and put them into these makeshift bags."

Family Struggles and Rejection

According to Texas Prison records, Williams was born Annie Laurie Havill in Hammond, Indiana, in 1922. She was the third of four children. Her father, a mechanical engineer, died when she was eleven.

At the time of the murders, her oldest brother, a civil engineer, said he had not heard from his sister for 16 years except for a phone call shortly before she was arrested.

"For my part, I want nothing to do with her in any way or fashion," he added.

Williams's sister stated, "Of course, we love her very much and can't understand how all of this trouble could have happened. Anything I could do to help, I would be more than happy to."

But Williams' younger brother wrote that she was "a very selfish personality as a child. Self-centered. I would prefer no contact between myself and this member of my family. We wish to protect our small children and guard against the emotional disturbance of knowledge of this terrible crime."

Williams was married and divorced in 1940.

She graduated from high school in Smithville, Tennessee, as an honor roll student in 1941.

Teachers recommended Williams for business school, but she could not afford it. After graduation, she worked for a year and a half in a pants factory.

Williams became a clerk at Piggly Wiggly grocery store, where she also became a manager trainee. She quit because the manager quote, "kept bothering me."

Williams spent the next year and a half working at a Ford Motor Company plant building B-24 Bombers for World War II.

It was here that she met and later married Hoyt J. Williams, who was attending an Air Force school near the plant.

A Marriage Marked by Trouble

A feature story published in December of 1936 in *The Tampa Daily Times* described how then teenager Hoyt Williams of Mulberry, Florida, had won a model airplane contest for the longest flight of the day.

The newspaper stated that "his plane thrilled the spectators by staying up two minutes and eight seconds and going a distance of nearly a half-mile."

26-year-old Hoyt and 22-year-old Annie married in Tampa, Florida, on February 19th of 1945.

During the next year, the couple moved to Army Air Force bases in Denver, West Palm Beach, Nashville, and Manchester, New Hampshire.

Their first child, Calvin, was born in Manchester on October 22, 1945. Two weeks later, her husband Hoyt went AWOL, absent without leave. This was shortly after Japan surrendered, ending World War II.

The couple and their newborn fled to Smithville, Tennessee, where Annie's mother lived.

Nine months later, on August 10, 1946, FBI agents and state police officers showed up at Williams' trailer home to arrest her husband for desertion.

Annie, who was pregnant at the time with their second son, Conrad, fired 50 shots at the officers. Her husband was imprisoned for 15 months and released in February 1947.

In September of 1950, back in Smithville, Tennessee, Hoyt Williams crashed a biplane into five cars, injuring 15 people while performing stunts at an air show.

He suffered a fractured skull, among other injuries, and was charged with reckless flying.

After his recovery, the couple and their two boys bounced around every two to six weeks, drilling irrigation wells. Hoyt now worked as a welder.

The Road to Addiction

Annie Williams told investigators that she began using Seconol, widely abused prescription sleeping pills from Mexico, to relieve pain from a cesarean section during the birth of her second son.

Williams claimed she never became addicted to the widely abused prescription sleeping aid and used them for rest when needed.

But in the 1950s and 60s, Seconol was known on the street as "red devils" or "reds."

People abused it to feel a mild euphoria, lack of inhibition, and relief of anxiety.

After her arrest for the murders, Williams claimed that she gave her sons an overdose of Seconal sleeping capsules.

The family moved into a house trailer near Galveston, Texas, in the summer of 1954. A few months later, the FBI arrested Hoyt Williams for transporting a stolen car across state lines in West Virginia four years earlier.

He was sentenced to three years and sent to the federal penitentiary in Atlanta, Georgia.

Williams and her two boys moved to a trailer home in Pasadena. She later told investigators, "My life with my husband was not a happy one and had not been for the last nine years."

She said her husband kept sending letters from prison that blamed her for their problems and that she was "no good."

Williams said she decided to "take her kids and leave and just disappear."

She rented an apartment in Houston and paid a month's rent of $50 in advance on Sunday, February 13, 1955.

A Mother's Murderous Resolve

Three days later, upset after receiving two letters from her husband, Williams said, "I decided to kill my two children and myself."

She put her plans into motion at 8 PM on February 16th. Williams claimed she substituted an overdose of Seconal sleeping capsules for cold medicine, gave it to the boys, and went to bed.

However, an autopsy revealed fractured skulls. Williams had bludgeoned her sons to death.

Williams gave a lengthy confession to a Texas Ranger and a Harris County Sheriff's Deputy on February 23, 1955.

A Cold and Detached Confession

In a detached, matter-of-fact tone, Williams never referred to her sons by their names as she confessed.

They were in their beds.

The oldest one was lying on his stomach and the youngest one on his back, and the youngest one was partly uncovered.

And I thought he was dead, but I wasn't sure, but I didn't want to do anything with them unless I was sure.

I looked at the youngest one and I felt of him and he felt cool and I couldn't feel his heart beating and the bed was wet.

When I thought I saw his stomach move, but I couldn't be sure and I got a man's handkerchief and tied around his neck and put a nail in it and twisted it.

While I was twisting on the nail, he never did move and I decided he was dead.

Then I went to examine the other boy, the older one, and I felt under his heart, and I couldn't feel anything.

I put the same handkerchief around his neck, put the same nail in it, and twisted.

After I decided they were dead, I thought about taking some more pills myself, but I thought of the disgrace of it, and I decided not to kill myself.

I decided to take them over to the apartment that I had rented, I thought I would take them over and figure out some way to dispose of their bodies.

I put them in my Cadillac, took them over to the apartment before daylight. I put them in the backseat of the Cadillac.

I took them from the backseat of the car and took them upstairs to the apartment myself.

I don't know which one I took up there first. They were not real stiff and they were not real limp, either.

When I took the first one up to the apartment, I put him in the bathtub. And then I went downstairs and got the other one and put him in the bathtub too.

At that time, each of them had T-shirts and jeans on.

After I got the second one upstairs. I took their clothes off while they were in the bathtub, and then I turned the water on.

I got an idea that I could put something on them to dissolve them.

After daylight I went back to Pasadena in the Cadillac, and I had to stay around there long enough for the stores to open.

I then bought some lime, 10 pounds, at Browns store, which is a feed store.

I think it was 35, or 45 cents I paid for the lime, and that I took the lime back to the apartment.

When I got back with this lime. I poured it in the bathtub over the boys. There was still water in the bathtub at that time.

I checked the bodies and found that the lime did not seem to be dissolving or destroying the bodies of my two boys.

So on Friday morning. I went to the King Cole food market on Telephone road and bought a can of lye.

I then took the can of lye back to my apartment and poured this over the bodies of my two boys. And I went to bed.

I took some sleeping capsules and slept for some time.

I woke up at about 11 AM Saturday, I realized that the lye and the lime I had put on the bodies of my two children was not going to dissolve or destroy their bodies.

A bad odor was beginning to come from the bodies of my boys, and I knew that I was going to have to do something, or people would discover them by the odor.

I decided on Saturday to cut the bodies up and put them in the refrigerator to stop the odor. And so I would have more time to think.

I knew that I could not get the bodies of my two children in the refrigerator.

On Saturday, I bought some plastic by the yard from Grants on Main Street. And I bought this plastic in the basement, and I bought three yards.

I took this plastic back to my apartment on Clay Street, used a needle and thread, and made several plastic bags.

It was either late Saturday the 19th or Sunday the 20th of February, 1955, that I started cutting up the bodies of my two boys so that I could get the parts of their bodies into the plastic bags that I had made.

I tried to use a butcher knife to cut up the two boys, but it was too dull.

I then used two razor blades, which were double edge blades, (Blue Blades).

I worked at this for some time, two or three hours, and then I finished, I put the various parts of the bodies into plastic bags and then I put all of these plastic bags into the refrigerator.

About daylight. I took some more pills and went back to sleep and slept until almost dark on Sunday.

When I got up Monday I could smell a strong odor coming from the kitchen.

And I decided I needed a different car to carry the bodies away in, so I went down and I bought a 1948 Studebaker from Irby Motor Company on Fannin Street.

I paid $30 down on this car, which left me owing $220. The man told me I could pay $10 a week on the car.

I gave the name of Dena Linden but gave the Clay street address.

After I bought the Studebaker car, I went back to the town and bought some plastic bags that were already made, two sheets, a suitcase, some tweezers, face powder, thread, and a can opener.

I stated previously that I bought the plastic and other things that I've mentioned at Grants. I think this is correct, but it could have been Woolworth's store on Main Street.

After the above-mentioned stuff, I went to the apartment, drank some buttermilk, went to bed, and listened to the radio for a while.

A Macabre Disposal Plot

Williams awoke the next morning and put the four packages of body parts into the trunk of the Studebaker.

She drove for a half hour in the stench-filled car to the Johnson Motor Service and Wrecking Yard in Algoa, located south of Houston near Galveston.

Mr. and Mrs. Morris Johnson recognized Williams from an earlier visit when her husband had overhauled their 1950 Cadillac there before he went off to federal prison.

Williams told the couple she had some spoiled deer meat in the car.

She claimed a friend's deep freeze had "gone on the blink" and needed to get rid of the venison because the deer had been shot illegally out of season.

Morris Johnson directed them to a vacant lot behind his wrecking yard.

Mrs. Johnson remarked that there was an awful odor in the Studebaker and that she would walk because she had a weak stomach.

But Annie Williams insisted that Mrs. Johnson ride in the car.

When they arrived at a ditch, Mr. Johnson opened the trunk lid.

Mrs. Johnson untied a large bundle wrapped in cloth inside the trunk. It contained four other bundles.

Little did they know it was the mutilated bodies of William's sons.

The first bundle contained the boy's legs with feet attached; arms, forearms, and hands; thighs, legs, and feet.

The second bundle in a cardboard box contained a woman's black coat, slip, and panties.

- A small boy's shirt and socks which had been cut off.

- A large boy's shirt and socks which had been cut off.

- Both boy's pairs of blue jeans.

- A matching pair of a child's thighs that had been removed at the hip and knee joints, neatly wrapped in newspaper from the Houston Chronicle dated Sunday, February 20, 1955.

The third bundle contained the red-haired, blue-eyed head and trunk of one boy partially covered in lime. The left side of his head, face, and upper arms showed trauma.

An autopsy revealed that contrary to Williams' claim that she had killed the boys with sleeping capsules, both had been bludgeoned to death. They had suffered fractured skulls and broken jaws.

The fourth bundle contained the head and trunk of a smaller boy dusted in lime. His head and face were fractured and swollen.

Mrs. Johnson, unaware of what was in the bundles, threw three of them into a ditch.

When she started to get the fourth bundle out of the trunk, Annie Williams stopped her.

Williams claimed it contained a box of bloody Kotex feminine napkins.

Williams herself placed the bundle into the ditch with the other three.

Mr. Johnson said he was busy and would cover up the bundles later.

Annie Williams drove Mrs. Johnson back to the house where they lived in the wrecking yard.

They left the doors of the Studebaker wide open to air out the foul odor. Williams said she was hungry, and they went inside to eat.

During the meal, Morris Johnson came in and asked Williams about her husband. She claimed he was working in Florida and didn't reveal that he was in prison.

Williams told Johnson her sons were home watching a new TV.

By late afternoon, Annie Williams insisted they return to the vacant lot to bury the bundles they had thrown into the ditch.

She said she wasn't going to leave until the bundles were covered because she did not want dogs to scatter the contents all over the neighborhood.

Mrs. Johnson suggested that her 19-year-old grandson Clayton and his seven-year-old brother, Butch, get shovels and help Williams cover the bundles with dirt.

When the seven-year-old kept asking what was inside the bundles, Williams became irritated and told him to go home.

After covering up the bundles, Williams ate dinner with the Johnsons and their grandson Clayton.

And after dinner, Williams dropped Clayton off at a movie theater in nearby Alvin.

The Grim Discovery

When Clayton came out of the theater at around 9 PM, he saw a story on the front page of the Houston Press newspaper that Williams and her two sons had been reported missing from Pasadena five days earlier.

A fellow employee at a Krutes Five and Dime store had told Pasadena police that she became worried when Annie Williams didn't show up for work. Williams had given her a letter with instructions to open it if anything ever happened to her. Inside, Williams's co-worker found a blank check with a note to look after the boys and keys to her Cadillac and house trailer.

Clayton Johnson said when he saw the newspaper story about Williams missing, he "put two and two together." He and a friend drove back to his grandparents' wrecker yard and dug up the bundles.

Shining their flashlight into the ditch, they discovered the boy's arms and legs. And called the police.

At 4 AM on Wednesday, February 23rd, Harris County Sheriff C.V. "Buster" Kern and his deputies broke down the door of Williams' apartment.

Sheriff Kern said she had a loaded pistol but made no attempt to use it.

The Arrest and Astrology Obsession

The Sheriff found her apartment littered with dozens of books and magazines about astrology and many horoscopes cast by Mrs. Williams on her own life.

The latest horoscope, found on top of her dresser, included the notation: "Extra caution. Steady and slow until the 27th."

When her murder trial opened on November 7, 1955, Williams was pictured smiling and holding hands with a woman identified as her spiritual advisor.

In her confession, Williams stated,

I realized that I had done a terrible thing--made a terrible mistake. But after I had done it. I had to go through with it.

When I say, I had to go through with it. I mean that I had to dispose of those two bodies. The handkerchief that I used to strangle my two boys with, I flushed down the toilet in the trailer courts, after I had cut it up.

I put the nail back in the drawer, and as far as I know it is still there in the trailer at Pasadena.

I put the razor blades in the garbage can at my apartment on Clay Street.

There was nobody that had anything to do with it, nobody helped me, and nobody knew anything about it as far as I know.

I don't feel sorry for myself, but I feel sorry for all the people I have hurt.

Sheriff Kern told the press that after confessing, Williams broke down and sobbed, "take me to the electric chair! I don't care anymore now!"

Annie Williams, arrest and confession, was front page news across the nation.

From federal prison, Hoyt J. Williams defended his wife, stating, "I have always loved my wife and children, and I still love my wife. I understand she has made a statement but if she did anything wrong, she was not responsible. My desire is to stand by her and assist her in any way possible."

A reporter for *The Baytown Sun* went to the dimly lighted trailer camp, where he found two small bicycles leaning against the aluminum trailer home where the young victims had lived with Annie Williams.

Inside a tiny room, he found two small bunk beds similar to those in ships attached to each side of the trailer wall. It looked like boys had just crawled out from beneath the covers.

Book satchels with each boy's name, Calvin and Conrad, were penciled on each.

A storage compartment above one bed held toy cowboy gloves, pistols, and holsters.

A bookshelf held copies of "Young Readers Horse Stories" and "Young Readers Mystery Stories."

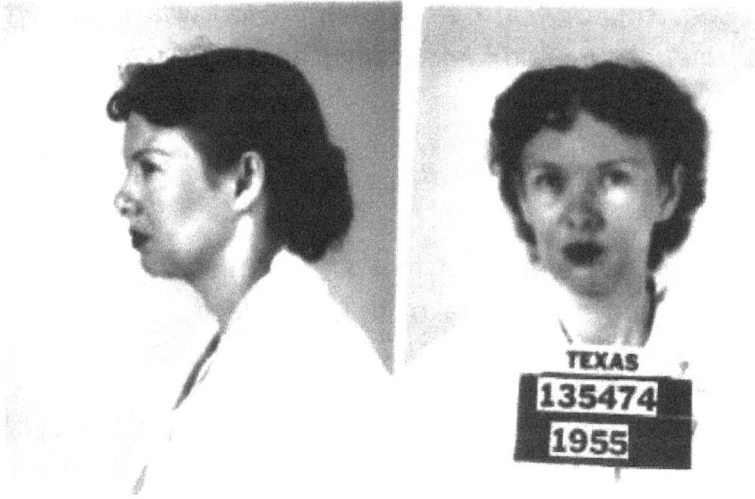

Annie Williams 1955 Mug Shot

The owner of the trailer camp said the boys played cowboys all the time with his 8-year-old son.

His impression of Annie Williams was, "She was just as nice. You couldn't ask for a better mother or lady."

Found Sane to Stand Trial

A county psychiatrist found Williams legally sane to stand trial.

The doctor said he asked Mrs. Williams if she wanted to attend funeral services for her sons, and she said no, telling him, "People will go to that funeral like people go to the zoo-- to see something curious. I don't want to have anything to do with it."

She told the psychiatrist that she killed her children because her sons were always being taunted about having a convict for a father. "People would say things about us, and the other kids would taunt the children. I couldn't stand to see them suffer anymore."

On November 8, 1955, Annie Laurie Williams, flanked by famed criminal defense attorney Percy Forman, pleaded guilty to killing and dismembering her boys, Conrad, 8, and Calvin, 9.

Mrs. Williams replied that she had no comment "whatever" after the judge asked her if she had anything to say before being sentenced.

She was sentenced to serve not less than two years and not more than life on each charge.

The District Attorney told the press Williams would not become eligible for parole for 34 years.

But Williams would receive parole 25 years later.

A New Story Emerges

After the trial, the 33-year-old convicted killer, in a jail house interview, claimed her attorney Percy Foreman had sold her down the river.

Williams now claimed an unidentified man had killed her sons and forced her to bury their mutilated remains.

Williams had found God while she was in jail there. She was baptized in the Baptist faith.

As she departed the Harris County Jail for the Texas Prison System, she cheerfully wished the jailers goodbye and good luck.

Interviewed on her arrival at the Texas Prison System in Huntsville in November of 1955, Williams now claimed her husband Hoyt had hired a hitman who killed the boys and forced her to bury their mutilated bodies.

During the interview, Williams was described as anxious and wanted to know, "What's the shortest time I could make parole."

A prison doctor stated during two interviews, "The subject is shy, and would answer only the questions asked. She would not refer to her children by name--referring to them only as "my boys" or the "oldest boy." She seems shy. Not at all guilty laden, he concluded.

The prison system gave Williams a rehabilitative rating of Fair to Very Poor.

Nine years later, Williams' husband, the man who defended his wife from the federal penitentiary, the man Williams later claimed had hired a hitman to kill their children, the man she tried to protect in a gun battle to keep FBI agents from arresting him for desertion, the man who crashed a stunt plane into a crowd of spectators at an airshow, was in the cockpit of an airplane being pursued by fighter jets from the Egyptian Air Force.

In 1964, at the controls of a Texas oilman's twin-engine transport plane, Williams ignored repeated orders to land according to the Egyptian government.

Williams and a Swiss mechanic had been making mysterious flights from Jordan to Libya for some time.

As Williams was about to leave the country's airspace, a burst of machine-gun fire ripped through his aircraft. A few days later, searchers recovered his body from the mud of the Nile Delta.

Unbeknownst to Annie Williams, sitting in prison back in Texas, Hoyt Williams had remarried three months before the deadly crash, and his new wife was pregnant.

Released On Parole

In 1980, after serving only 25 years of the life sentence for the murder and mutilation of her young sons, the Texas Parole Board released Annie Williams.

It was a time of revolving door justice when the Texas prison system was more interested in relieving overcrowding than protecting the public.

Williams moved to the Path Seekers Halfway House in Houston, which was located near the Astrodome.

She earned $379.63 monthly as an office aide on a work release program.

In September of 1981, with less than nine months left to serve on parole, 59-year-old Annie Williams went on a date with a man for dinner and never returned.

During three earlier outings, she had withdrawn a total of $2,225 from her bank account.

Three wigs were missing from her room. The halfway house supervisor stated, "Annie was a very private person during her stay with us, and she did not let us know anything more than she wanted us to know.

Williams vanished for 16 years.

Fugitive Hunter Louis Fawcett Catches the Case

Louis Fawcett, Investigator Office of Inspector General, TDCJ 1997

It was then that her case landed on the desk of Louis Fawcett, known as one of Texas' most tenacious and persistent fugitive hunters.

Fawcett's phone rang on March 26th, 1997.

"I got a telephone call from the Department of Public Safety, their fugitive unit. And they told me that this fugitive, an elderly woman, by now, most wanted for murder and her two little boys back in the 50s. And told me the gruesome story, how she'd cut them up, put them to sleep, and what she actually did to them. And that's how I got on the case."

State police told Fawcett that a woman named Annie Laurie Williams, with the exact birthdate as their fugitive, had renewed her driver's license in Garland, a suburb of Dallas.

A few minutes later, Fawcett knocked on a door expecting to make an arrest. The woman who answered had the same name and exact date of birth, but it turned out to be a case of mistaken identity.

"We asked her if she would go with us down to the police department to get fingerprinted. She said this is not the first time this has happened to me. I'd be happy to go down there. She was very cooperative. We fingerprinted her and compared the prints, but it wasn't her. That's when I really cranked it up. I got a hold of the records, prison records, and saw the offense and what she'd done to those children. And I made it a priority to get her back in prison.

Fawcett knew that some fugitives often reestablished a new life using an alias. He ran Williams' social security number through the system.

"I found out that her social security number was linked to another social security number under another woman's name.

She was drawing benefits from a deceased man. So I knew then that she was living off somebody else's Social Security check.

Reinventing Herself in Idaho

In April 1985, four years after absconding from parole in Texas, Williams married James Allen in Riggins, Idaho.

Allen had recently lost his leg, his wife, and his oldest son. Residents of the small town of 600 remembered Williams, known as Laurie Allen, as a quiet person. She was especially fond of her dog, who she walked several times daily.

Williams' husband had died of an apparent heart attack shortly after they married.

U.S. Marshals arrested the 75-year-old Williams at the Irwin Retirement Center in Riggins.

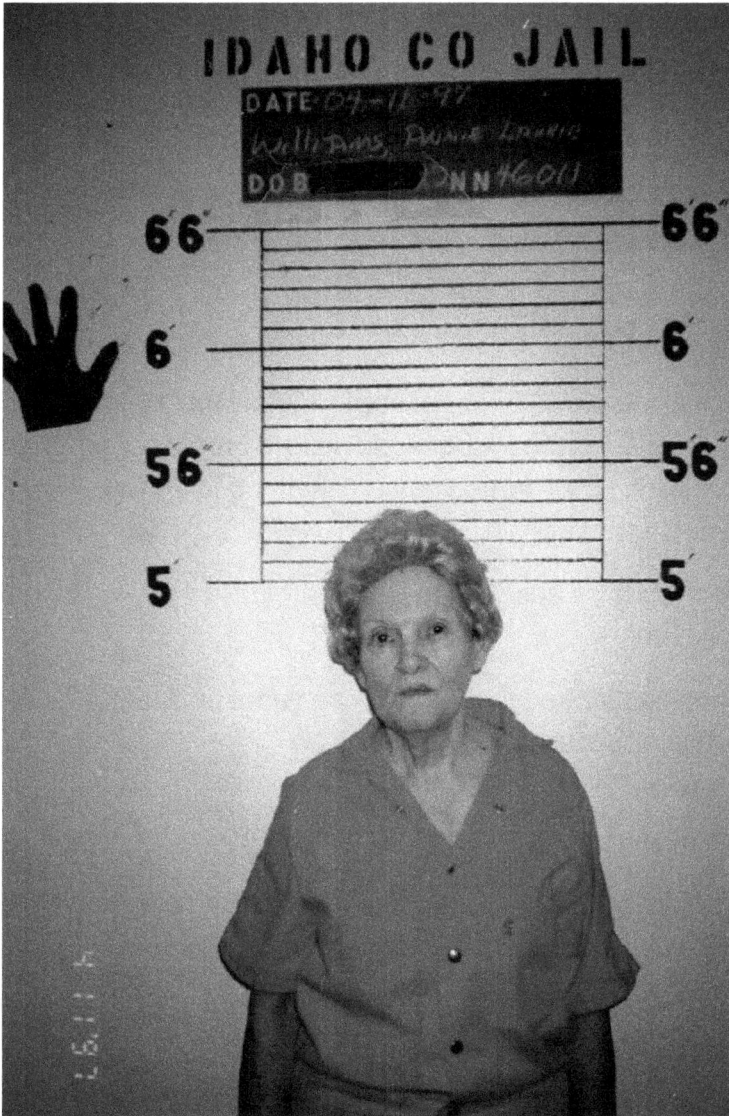

Annie Williams 1997 Booking Mug Shot

After Williams was apprehended, her late husband's sister questioned the cause of his death. She told the Associated Press that her brother "was in his mid-60s and considered himself a very healthy man until then. Williams was hard to get acquainted with. She didn't make friends easily."

Fawcett says Williams' social security fraud scheme started at the nursing home where she met and married James Allen, a fellow resident. "And about two weeks after they got married, he died. So she applied for his benefits rights, thinking that she was clear because she wasn't using her own social security number."

Fawcett says the death was mysterious and believes that despite her age, Williams was capable of murder.

In news interviews after her capture, Williams claimed she fled the Houston halfway because fellow parolees called her a "baby killer." She denied having anything to do with murdering and dismembering her sons.

When Williams absconded from parole, Texas did not have a fugitive unit.

No one had looked for her all those years until the case landed on Fawcett's desk.

Paroled Again

Three years after U.S. Marshals returned Williams to prison, the Texas Parole Board released her on December 6, 2000.

Twelve years later, Williams died in a nursing home in Central Texas at 90 years of age.

Louis Fawcett retired from hunting fugitives in 2018.

Fawcett, a baby boomer and child of the fifties, says this case was personal.

He identified with the young victims. Saturday morning TV westerns featured the adventures of *The Lone Ranger*, *Roy Rogers*, and *Davy Crockett* at the Alamo.

Boys in rural Texas idolized cowboy heroes. Residents remembered the Williams brothers, in cowboy hats and holstered six-shooters, pedaling around the trailer court.

Their bikes were their horses in an imaginary posse on the trail of bad guys. Unfortunately, there were no heroes to protect them from a mother with murder and malice in her heart.

In 1955, the shocked and grief-stricken community took up a collection to bury the murdered brothers in Alvin. Police recovered their mutilated body parts in the Johnson wrecking yard a short drive from there.

A pair of large ornate pink granite headstones mark their graves in the Oak Park Cemetery. 8-year-old Conrad S. Williams. And his brother, 9-year Calvin H. Williams, rest side by side.

Headstones of 8-year-old Conrad Williams & 9-year-old Calvin Williams, Oak Park Cemetery - Alvin, Texas

67

Green mold grows on Calvin's headstone. Vandals tipped over Conrad's headstone. It lies flat on the ground.

Piles of scattered brown leaves and broken tree limbs cover the boy's graves. Few remember the terrible end to their short lives that made front page headlines here.

But veteran Texas lawman Louis Fawcett, the fugitive hunter who always got his man or woman, says it is the one case out of hundreds that will never fade from his memory.

Epilogue

I received a note from a family member who wrote:

"This woman was my grandfather's sister. She was disowned by him, and no one spoke about her. I learned about her through my mother and only started researching her after his passing. My mother remembers playing with her cousins and then never seeing them again – only to learn about what happened to them years later."

I also received this message from a woman who became friends with Williams after she was released on parole in December of 2000.

She wrote:

"I knew Annie very, very well. Believe it or not, despite what she did, she was really a very nice lady. She was paroled to my best friend, and she lived in the house with us. Annie and I used to talk about poetry, books, and old movies, and she shared stories of how she helped make airplanes during WWII. I took her to do her shopping, to doctor appointments, and out to lunch. She needed help shopping and various tasks because she was legally blind. All she could see was the outlines of people, but not faces.

She fascinated me so much because she was highly intelligent with an above-average IQ. It was hard to believe she committed a crime so heinous because the Annie I came to know was not capable of such a crime. She was a different person after she did all that time in prison or maybe she had multiple personalities. I didn't see any evidence of that, but I'm not a doctor. My friend and I had to put her in a nursing home in Hearne, Texas, back in 2007 or 2008 because she became confused and somewhat combative."

Four years after her parole, at age 85, Annie Williams, the mother who shocked the nation by brutally hacking up her 9-year-old son Calvin and his 8-year-old brother Conrad, died on April 9, 2012.

Closing the chapter of one of the most cold-blooded crimes in Texas history.

Dialing From Death Row

The last place you would expect to receive a cell phone call from is Death Row.

Yet, serial killer Richard Tabler, a condemned killer awaiting execution by lethal injection, started dialing for terror.

Tabler's audacious use of a smuggled cell phone to threaten a Texas Senator ignited a political firestorm, unmasking a glaring security breach within the prison system.

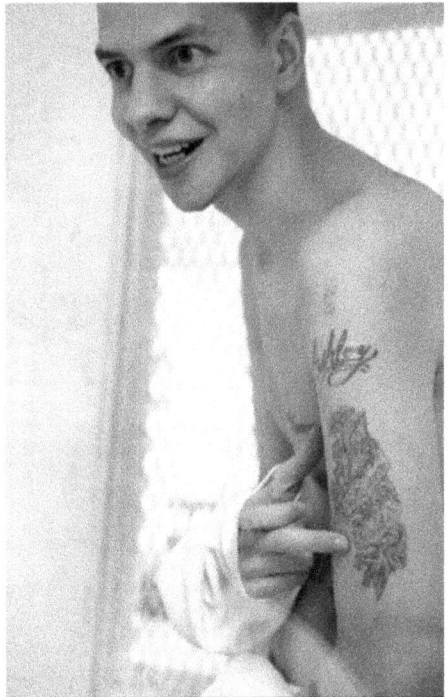

Richard "Blue" Tabler
Texas Death Row Inmate

Across the U.S., prisoners wielding illegal cell phones orchestrate a web of threats and criminal enterprises from behind bars.

Richard Tabler is a bizarre, cold-blooded serial killer who recruited an Army private as his accomplice.

And Tabler, it turns out, was a police drug informant.

In a typewritten letter to me, Tabler claimed he had found religion.

When you finish reading this, tell me if you believe him.

Death Row Inmate Threatens Powerful Senator

Tabler became the investigative target of John Moriarty, the Inspector General for the Texas Department of Criminal Justice after the serial killer got his hands on a contraband cell phone to threaten a Texas Senator.

John Moriarty, Inspector General - TDCJ

"It's an epidemic, you know, the cell phones inside are a huge threat to the security of the institution. And they can call a victim or run a criminal enterprise from inside."

A seizure at the maximum security Polunsky prison unit in Texas underscores the problem.

Officers confiscated 30 Samsung Galaxy cell phones and chargers hidden inside a long hollowed-out wood beam.

Cell Phones Confiscated at Texas Death Row

It arrived in a load of wood shipped from a Home Depot in Houston to be donated to the prison's craft shop.

The Office of Inspector General arrested a couple who paid for the shipment.

The Polunsky Unit also houses Texas Death Row inmates. It was here in 2008, that serial killer Richard Tabler set off a political firestorm by using a smuggled cell phone to threaten a Texas lawmaker.

John Whitmire, the Texas State Senate's Criminal Justice Committee chairman, received a shocking phone call. "I know your daughters' names," a man warned. "I know how old they are. I know where they live." Then, in a chilling tone, the caller revealed the young women's names, ages, and addresses.

Senator Whitmire said the call scared the Hell out of him. And it should have.

Richard Tabler is a wild-eyed serial killer nicknamed "Blue."

Tabler was convicted of capital murder in the 2004 Thanksgiving holiday weekend killings of two men and two teenage girls in Killeen, the home of Fort Hood now named Fort Cavazos. His accomplice was a soldier from the base who videotaped the murders.

John Moriarty recalls Tabler's strange behavior. "It just something wasn't right with him.Two minutes into a conversation and you could tell this guy's a bubble off. He was definitely a bizarre, dangerous individual.

During the cell phone call, Senator Whitmire heard the distinct sound of prison noise in the background. Tabler held up the phone and asked, 'Did you hear that?' and replied, 'That's a prison.'

Whitmire questioned how Tabler got the phone. The death row inmate boldly replied that he paid $2,100 and even had a charger.

It was the first of a series of calls Tabler made to the powerful senator complaining about living conditions on Death Row.

In response, Texas locked down the 155-thousand inmates in its prison system and conducted a massive search for contraband cell phones across 112 prison units.

Corrections officers discovered nineteen other illegal cell phones on Death Row and hundreds more across the system.

Death Row was supposed to be the system's most secure prison. Inmates are confined to individual cells for 23 hours a day.

They are kept isolated from other inmates when guards escort them out to shower and to a recreation cage for one hour a day.

A month before he threatened the Senator, Tabler racked up 2,800 minutes on his cell phone and shared it with nine other prisoners on Death Row.

The incident in 2008 revealed a new security problem or remote control drones that Moriarty says plagues U.S. prisons to this day. "We caught gang members that were using these drones to drop in mainly narcotics. In some of the facilities, people would park nearby and then walk near the perimeter fences of the prison and throw contraband over.

Moriarty traced the purchase of the cell phone used by Tabler to a store in Waco, Texas, and 44 calls made on it to the home phone number of his mother in Georgia.

Police arrested 60-year-old Lorraine Tabler when she arrived at the Austin airport to visit her son. She had been buying time for the phone.

Tabler had nothing to lose. As a death row inmate once defiantly told me, "What are you going to do? Kill me?"

Tabler had already asked a judge to end his appeals and schedule his execution.

"He's a bizarre individual. I would really like to read a psychiatric report, because I have never even heard of anybody attempting to do something like that. From the start, he said, put me to death, recalled Bell County Sheriff's Deputy Tim Steglich.

Steglich investigated Tabler's murder spree.

A Serial Killer's Past and Bizarre Behavior

Tabler, known as "Blue," rolled into Killeen from Los Angeles in 2004, a few months after his release from a California prison, where he served his second sentence in four years for burglary and forgery.

Tabler called his first trip to prison "Gladiator School."

Arriving in Killeen, he lived with his mother and sister, sleeping on his mother's bedroom floor or with a girlfriend.

Tabler sold drugs at Fort Hood, the nation's largest Army Post. The convicted criminal routinely passed through security at its gate, dressed as a soldier using a fake military identification card.

"I think he liked playing roles. I can't tell you how many heads rolled in the Army over that, said Steglich.

A Deadly Partnership

Tabler met 18-year-old Timothy Doan Payne, an Army private from Missouri, at Fort Hood. They became inseparable.

Tabler and Payne hung out together at Teazers, one of the area's most popular topless bars located near the gate to the Army Post.

The cigarette smoke-filled bar catered to soldiers who played pool and watched the dancers.

A large American flag painted on an outside wall faced the parking lot.

Payne was a regular, generous tipper who always sat near the right side of the stage for a view of its stripper pole.

Timothy Payne Mug Shot TDCJ

Obsession with Teazers Topless Club

Tabler was a regular, initially popular with many dancers, installing stereos in some of their cars.

Tabler claimed he was a gang member and had a tattoo on his head to prove it. He also spun stories of being a CIA operative and bragged about his arsenal of guns.

Tabler, who was 25, became fixated on Amber Benefield, a 16-year-old dancer called Zoe.

He pestered the dancers. His behavior became downright creepy. He quickly wore out his welcome.

The bar's boisterous and popular Moroccan manager, 25-year-old Mohamed Amine Rahmouni, known as Amine, kicked Tabler out of the topless club.

The Hit List and Thanksgiving Revenge

Permanently banned from the bar, an enraged Tabler drew up a hit list of a dozen targets for revenge.

Richard Tabler launched his plot for revenge the day after Thanksgiving of 2004.

He was gunning for Amine, the manager who kicked him out of the Teazers, topless bar.

Permanently banned and with a bruised ego, Tabler decided to get back at the manager and the dancers who had made fun of him.

He lured Amine and his 28-year-old friend, Haitham Frank Zayed, a used car dealer facing assault charges, to a deserted parking lot with the prospect of buying stolen stereo equipment for $1500.

Tabler had set up a drug buy earlier for $500 in X pills and $500 in cocaine and owed the dealer cash.

He told his accomplice, Timothy Payne, the Army private, that he had no intention of selling anything. He was going to rob Amine and shoot him if he did not give up the money.

Tabler and Payne drove a borrowed pickup truck to the parking lot of an electric company located just outside the Killeen city limits.

At 2:30 AM, Amine rolled in with Zayed behind the wheel of their car.

Tabler walked up to the driver's side window. Started talking and demanded to see the money. When Zayed refused, Tabler shot him in the head and put a round into Amine, sitting beside him in the front passenger seat.

Tabler yelled at Payne to open the passenger car door. He told Payne to search Amine's pocket for money while he looked in Zayed's pockets.

During the search, Amine's head fell over on the sleeve of Payne's left arm. It spooked him, and he urged Tabler to leave.

Tabler was having none of that. He went to the passenger side and pulled Amine to the ground. Payne flipped the body onto its back so Tabler could search his pockets.

Then, Tabler told Payne to cut the seatbelt off the driver, Zayed. Payne started to freak out.

A Gruesome Videotaped Execution

Tabler told his accomplice to watch for cars. He pulled Zayed out of the vehicle and looked inside for money. None was to be found.

Next, a frustrated Tabler told Payne to get his video camera and start recording as he stood over Amine's body. As the tape rolled, Amine sputtered a gurgling sound from his lips and raised his hand.

Tabler looked at the body and proclaimed to the camera, "Who's got the power now." and squeezed off a 9mm round point blank into his head again. So close that blood splattered onto Tabler's pistol.

Tabler then stole a black bag out of the victim's car, and they drove off to his girlfriend's house.

When they arrived, she noticed that Payne's shirt had blood spots all over it. They calmly sat in her living room, watching the video. Afterward, Tabler threatened to kill her and Payne if they ever told anybody about what they saw on the tape.

The next day, they burned the tape and tried to wash evidence off the pickup truck.

Tim Steglich soon learned from the Killeen police that a man called "Blue" was a possible suspect. Blue was the nickname for one of their drug informants. None other than Richard Tabler, who dealt drugs at Fort Hood.

Steglich started digging into Tabler's criminal history.

"He had active felony warrants out of Florida, but it was a Thanksgiving weekend. I couldn't get those felony warrants confirmed. They were nonextraditable at the moment, so you couldn't necessarily take him into custody on that. But I knew we had a problem."

Without evidence that Tabler was involved in the murders, there was no probable cause to get an arrest warrant.

A New Plot to Silence Witnesses

Meanwhile, Tabler hatched a new murder plot, and Payne went along with it. Tabler suspected that two of the topless dancers at Teazers were spreading stories that he had killed their manager.

Two days after the Thanksgiving murders, Tabler and Payne lured the dancers to a remote state park with the promise to sell them cocaine. They were on the way to dance at a topless bar in Austin, driving a jeep owned by a boyfriend.

Tabler murdered 18-year-old Tiffany Lorraine Dotson, a pretty blonde dancer from California, and the fellow dancer he had fixated on,16-year-old Amanda Benefield, a 16-year-old, green-eyed red-haired runaway from Louisiana called Zoe.

After the murders, Tabler lost it when he heard that Steglich was on this trail.

Tim Steglich, Investigator Bell County Sheriff

"He was threatening to come to the Sheriff's office and start killing people. And he made a specific request to talk to me. So we had to station armed people throughout the Sheriff's office because it wasn't that secure. The doors were open at the front."

Steglich told dispatchers to keep Tabler talking the next time he called. Tabler called back and revealed there was a cigar at the murder scene, a fact never publically revealed. Now Steglich had probable cause to make an arrest.

The Interrogation and Confession

Once inside the interrogation room with Steglich, Tabler confessed. He thought all four murders were justified.

Steglich used a technique of getting into the personal space of the suspect.

"Tabler puts up a timeout sign. He says, timeout, I shot him. So, I reminded him of his rights again. He says, No, I don't want a lawyer. And he said, I also had a list of eight more people that I was going to kill."

Timothy Payne received a life sentence for his role in killing the strip club manager and his friend. Now 37, he will become eligible for parole in 2044.

Tabler was convicted of capital murder and was sentenced to death in March 2007.

Conviction and a Chilling Farewell

He had these parting words for Steglich. "I saw him when I went back into the jail for something, and they were moving him. And Tabler yells at me hey, Steglich, no hard feelings. And I just shook my head. I said, How in the world? Can you say something like that."

A few months later, Tabler sent threatening letters to Whitmire warning that he could get to him anywhere.

A 51-year-old Methodist Chaplain admitted to smuggling Tabler's letters out of the prison during a two-month period. He was supposed to be ministering to the prison's 2,900 convicts, including 328 men on death row.

Tabler agreed to do an interview with me but was forbidden to meet because of his disciplinary problems.

Claims of Redemption and Reflection

Forty-four years old as of 2024, Tabler replied in a typewritten letter to me, stating that he is working on a faith-based book for teens, stating, "The young man that did this horrible crime back in 2004 is not the same man that you want to interview here at the Polunsky Unit's Death Row. I just made a mistake and poor judgment and there is not a day that goes by that I don't beat myself up over it and wish that there was a rewind button so I could return to that night and walk away or be like Jesus and raise the dead, but I cannot.

It's impossible to know a man's heart and if he has truly repented. But there's an old saying that Jesus Christ must certainly live in the penitentiary because everybody finds him when they get there.

Tabler was executed by lethal injection on February 13, 2025 at 6:38 p.m. He gave a final statement as some of the families of his victims witnessed his execution.

"There is not a day that goes by that I don't regret my actions, I had no right to take your loved ones from you, and I ask and pray; hope and pray that one day you find it in your hearts to forgive me for those actions," Tabler said. "No amount of my apologies will ever return them to you."

A Defiant Outlaw's Ballad

Willie Nelson sings about riding a horse in the wide-open spaces of Texas with lyrics titled *"Don't Fence Me In"*.

"Don't Fence Me In" could be the ballad of Texas inmate Dennis Wayne Hope.

Hope bragged that there wasn't a prison in the state of Texas that could keep him behind bars.

And he almost proved it.

Hope blacked out the maximum security Darrington prison on Thanksgiving to make one of his many escapes.

The Historic Darrington Prison

Folklorist John Lomax and his son Alan recorded the music of African American convicts there during the Depression.

A 1934 recording captured a work song by a prisoner called Lightnin' Washington by his fellow inmates who said he could think faster than the warden.

They chant "It's a Long John" about escaping bondage.

The lyrics continue, "Well I wouldn't listen. I wouldn't listen. Got to run'in around. Got to run'in around. First thing I know. First thing I know. I was jailhouse-bound. I was jailhouse-bound."

Darrington was originally a Civil War-era plantation. Convict labor leased from the Texas Prison Commission supplanted slave labor.

85

In 1918, the Prison Commission purchased the 6,747-acre plantation located south of Houston.

Today, inmates still raise cows, pigs, and poultry and work in the fields, planting and harvesting crops.

"The Texas prison systems were self-sufficient. They grew their own food and raised their own cattle, sheep, and hogs. Back then, they had the third-largest hog operation in the world," said John Moriarty, the former Inspector General of the Texas Department of Criminal Justice. "It's not totally self-sufficient now, but changes have improved conditions.

In 1963, before racial desegregation, the prison housed white second-time offenders.

By the 1980s, Darrington, now called a maximum-security unit, held the leaders of violent prison gangs among its more than 1800 inmates.

In 1986, the prison system built a 12-foot-high gunwalk so that guards could keep a closer eye on inmates in the recreation yards.

Thanksgiving Prison Break

This brings us to the Thanksgiving holiday of 1994.

Saturday, November 26th. Darrington was on a skeleton security shift. Most of the unit's 425 guards were at home with their families.

Inmate Gregory Ott was inside the prison boiler room, filling a water sample for a daily test.

At about 9:05 PM, the doorbell to the room buzzed.

Ott assumed a guard was making rounds and pushed the button to open the electric lock.

Inmate Jason Montgomery pushed his way inside, followed by 26-year-old Dennis Wayne Hope.

Montgomery was serving a life sentence for attempted capital murder.

Hope was serving an 80-year sentence for armed robberies.

Hope grabbed Ott from behind. Put his arm around his neck. Forced him to the floor.

And said, "I was told to just kill you, but I've got nothing against you. Lie there and shut up, and you won't get hurt."

Hope and Montgomery tied Ott's hands behind his back and his legs with electrical wire.

And bound his hands with electrical tape.

They wanted to know if all of the prison lights would go out when the electric power was shut off.

Ott replied yes but was afraid the boiler would blow up.

Hope and Montgomery pulled green prison blankets out of their shirts and began tying the blankets around their legs.

The doorbell buzzed again. A third inmate, Harry Decker, showed up.

Decker was serving a life sentence for aggravated robbery.

The leggings made of blankets would help them get through razor wire on the prison fences.

They had also made dark clothing with hoods out of the blankets to cover their white prison uniforms.

Hope masterminded the escape plan.

But inmates Montgomery and Decker didn't know that Hope was using them to distract attention from his escape.

A Calculated and Fit Escape Artist

The blue-eyed, five-foot-eight-inch, 152-pound inmate had appeared to be a fitness fanatic. Doing hundreds of push-ups and handstands every day.

He calculated that ten laps around the prison recreation yard was a mile. He would run at least ten miles a day.

"He would run around the prison yard and move a small rock from one pocket to another to count one lap. He'd run 10 miles a day preparing for his escaped," recalled fugitive hunter Louis Fawcett.

Fawcett was a prison investigator assigned to the FBI Violent Crime Task Force in Dallas.

Fawcett specialized in hunting fugitives. Two weeks after joining the FBI squad, Dennis Hope became his first case.

A Life of Crime and Deception

Dennis Hope had been a grocery store stocker in Dallas. When he got passed over for a promotion, the 22-year-old retaliated.

He knew where money was kept and the schedule when armored cars would pick up daily deposits.

He robbed four supermarkets at gunpoint, some of the very ones where he had worked. He fired a round into one store and left.

In two other robberies, Hope dressed up in a uniform stolen from an armored car company.

He called a grocery store manager, telling him that the regular armored car was running late and that he was the substitute.

Hope walked out with $29,200 in cash from the first robbery and $37,000 in the second robbery.

The real armored cars rolled in shortly after Hope had made his getaway.

Later that month, a Dallas police detective spotted Hope wearing a shoulder holster with a Ruger 6 blue steel revolver in the Borrowed Money Bar nightclub parking lot.

Hope claimed he was a sheriff's deputy. He flashed a small badge with "special police officer" written on it and produced a pair of handcuffs.

The detective arrested him on the spot for impersonating an officer.

Behind bars in the Dallas County jail, Hope arrogantly demanded catered meals and a television for his cell.

An Escape Down Dallas Streets

Five months later, on his way to stand trial, Hope vanished from a line of prisoners who were handcuffed together at the Dallas County courthouse.

He used a key smuggled into the jail, hidden in his mouth, to get out of the cuffs.

Hope stripped off his white prison overalls down to his boxer shorts and jogged off through downtown Dallas.

Fawcett picks up the story of Hope's escape. "So he's running down the street when a policeman pulled up beside him and spoke to him. He said, I'm trying out for Triathlon officer. How are you today? Basically, just struck up a conversation. Didn't panic. Didn't run. Didn't fight any officers. Okay, the officer said well, have a nice day he drove off. He was very confident, very confident."

Four days later, Hope stole a Pontiac Trans Am from a service station when the driver left her keys in the ignition and went inside to pay. The next day, Hope got into a high-speed chase.

It ended when a State Trooper shot out the tires on his stolen car. Hope rationalized his robbery spree as "I needed the money."

In 1991, Hope was sentenced to 80 years in prison on four counts of aggravated robbery with a deadly weapon and four thirty-year sentences for stealing 20-grand dressed like an armored car guard, impersonating an officer, escape, and car theft.

Taking no chances, the Dallas County Sheriff transported Hope to the Texas Prison System Intake in Huntsville, Texas, wearing handcuffs, leg irons, and a belly chain.

He was sent to the Darrington Maximum Security Unit due to his high escape risk.

No Hope for Parole

Four years later, while watching TV in a prison recreation room, Hope saw a commercial for the gubernatorial campaign of George W. Bush.

When Bush was elected Governor of Texas on a law-and-order agenda he wrote to his mother that making parole was now hopeless.

Fawcett says that's when Hope put his escape plan in motion. "The Escape itself was very clever. I was determined that he was going to go or he was going to die in the process. I really believe that."

The Prison Blackout

After taking over the prison boiler room during Thanksgiving of 1994, Hope dashed toward the interior prison fence 100 feet away.

As Hope ran, Inmate Montgomery flipped off the master electrical switch. The maximum-security prison suddenly went dark.

Hope used pliers to cut a hole in the wire fence, went through it, and climbed over the exterior prison fence.

Inmates Montgomery and Decker were too weak to follow Hope over the fence.

They had to cut a hole in the wire, which slowed down their escape.

"They had trouble, and I think both of them were smokers. Dennis didn't smoke. And he was in shape. He had been preparing for it," said Fawcett.

The inmates had stolen pliers from the prison maintenance department, where inmates work as trustees.

At 9:30 PM, a guard in a picket tower 100 yards away saw inmates Decker and Montgomery running in the dark. He ordered them to halt and fired a warning shot with his rifle.

They briefly stopped and started running again. The guard fired four more rounds.

Decker fell to the ground, crying out that he had been shot in the foot. Montgomery crawled back to help him. Decker hadn't been shot. He had sprained his ankle.

The pair got up and started running again. The guard fired four more rounds but missed in the night.

Bloodhound Bait

John Moriarty says the prison turned loose its bloodhounds to find the inmates. Hope had set up inmates Decker and Montgomery to keep the dogs off his trail. "They were basically dog bait because he knew that the minute they went over the wire, the dogs would be put on the ground, and they would be tracking them."

Montgomery and Decker were caught on the prison grounds within a couple of hours.

A guard found inmate Montgomery lying flat on his back, covered with leaves, sticks, grass, and other brush.

When ordered to get up, Montgomery told the officer, quote, "I was just laying here thinking about blue skies and the Bahamas when your funky ass found me. I thought I had made it and was just about to roll me a cigarette."

Later, a captain of correctional officers who lived on the unit heard a noise outside his house. In the carport, he found inmate Decker leaning against the driver's side of his Ford van, dressed only in his inmate underwear and tennis shoes. When asked what he was doing, Inmate Decker responded, "I'm just watching," and he gave up.

A Foot Race to Freedom

Meanwhile, Dennis Wayne Hope was sprinting across the rural countryside. Fawcett said he was long gone. "He had found a church pamphlet that somebody had left at one of their services. It had a map that showed where the church was located relative to the prison. So when he hit the fence, he knew exactly what direction he would go."

Hope ran 8 miles at a fast clip. Swam across a canal. He rolled in the dirt to turn his white prison garb brown. And then ran 13 more miles to Pearland, Texas, south of Houston.

Hope lived off of hamburger buns thrown out from a McDonalds and hid in the weeds. He watched a service station for the next customer to leave keys in the ignition.

When the driver of a GMC pickup truck went inside to pay the cashier. Hope slipped behind the wheel. He had a long head start on fugitive hunter John Moriarty.

Creatures of Habit

"We set up a large command center operation in Huntsville, conducting interviews of cellmates and employees and trying to get any piece of the information that we can about his possible whereabouts. But one thing I've learned over the years is that these guys are creatures of habit. So the first thing we do is look at the case files to see what the escapee did in the past because he will go back to what he did without a doubt."

Hope proved to be a creature of habit. He headed back home to Rockwall, a suburb of Dallas.

In Mesquite, another suburb, Hope dumped the stolen pickup at a convenience store. He approached an 82-year-old man in the parking lot claiming that he had sprained his ankle and needed a ride.

Several blocks away, as the good samaritan neared his home, Hope pulled out a hunting knife to carjack him.

"The elderly gentleman tried to grab the knife and grab the blade. Dennis pulled the knife in his hand and cut it. He told him I'm not trying to hurt you; I just need a ride," said Fawcett.

Hope took the man's wallet with 80 dollars inside and dropped him off on the side of the road. For the next several days, he lived inside the car and would eat at McDonalds.

He purchased a BB pistol at a sporting goods store near the Borrowed Money Nightclub, where he had been arrested four years earlier for impersonating a sheriff's deputy.

Hope truly was a creature of habit. And that would play to the advantage of Moriarty and Fawcett, who were hot on his trail.

Hope used the BB gun to rob one of the grocery stores that he had originally been convicted of robbing. He brazenly entered the store even though a marked Irving Police patrol car was parked in front.

Hope held up a clerk for $1300 and calmly walked past the police officer. He drove his carjacked vehicle to a vantage point.

He watched and laughed as the grocery store's employees ran outside to tell the officer in the parked patrol car that they had been robbed. It was payback.

Fawcett says Hope felt he was treated unfairly when he had received 80 years for his earlier robberies. "He wasn't gonna do that time. He didn't feel like he earned that time. He didn't feel like he deserved that time for a little case of robbery. He said he didn't hurt anybody. And, of course, my response to that is if you put a gun on a young girl, you've hurt her. Because she's terrified, that will affect the rest of her life. But that was his attitude. He didn't hurt anybody. No harm, no foul, so to speak."

A Man of Three Lives

Investigators launched a statewide dragnet for Hope immediately after his escape. Crimestoppers posted an award. Wanted posters were distributed to grocery stores across the Dallas metropolitan area.

Investigators followed up on dozens of leads and sightings of Hope.

They interviewed ex-wives, ex-girlfriends, family members, friends, work associates, and his fellow inmates.

One woman told them that Hope lived three different lives:

1. Husband and Christian Image
2. Rich man's son to his girlfriends.
3. Top Thief in Town

Moriarty says part of Hope's motive for returning was to thumb his nose at the police.

"We are all creatures of habit but especially convicts. That's how they made their living before. They didn't get caught for all of them. They didn't get prosecuted for all of them. But they go back to what they know. In his case, he worked scams, being involved in picking up money from grocery stores dressed as a guard on an armored car. He would surveil them. He would know their times and know their routines because of his prior experience. The ability to obtain the money without having to kill anyone or shoot anyone, that's kind of what he did."

Thumbing His Nose at The Law

A dozen FBI surveillance teams staked out grocery stores with this order from their supervisor. "Given our boy's history, it should go without saying that you ensure you have a full tank of gas. He likes to travel at high rates of speed and for long distances. Please wear your vests and have your raid jacket handy in case we get rolling and have the occasion to get out on foot. I am certain there will be an overabundance of plainclothes detectives, and I don't want any identity mistakes.

SWAT teams set up on the tops of buildings and parking garages, but Hope never showed. He would case the grocery stores looking for the FBI stakeouts. Then, Hope would hit a grocery store nearby that was not under surveillance.

After committing the first grocery store robbery, Hope headed to Memphis, Tennessee.

He would use Memphis as his home base to commute back and forth to Dallas to commit more armed robberies.

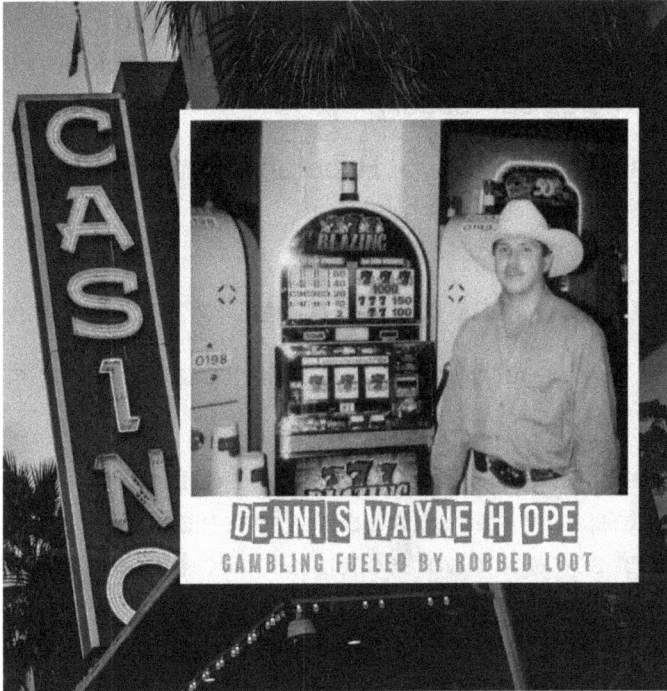

Dennis Wayne Hope gambling robbery proceeds at casino in Tunica, Mississippi

In Memphis, he was charming women and spending thousands of dollars from the robberies at casinos in Tunica, Mississippi, a short drive south of Memphis.

Life Imitates Art

Taking a scene from the movie *Cool Hand Luke*, Hope sent letters and fifty-dollar money orders to his friends back at the Darrington Prison unit. He bragged about his cool life outside in what inmates call the "free world."

He signed one as Your Bro. Dangerous "D". On another letter, the return address in Hope's handwriting was Irk Megclerk from 1269 Drop Trousers, Austin, Texas.

Another letter contained the PS message: Big Bank Hank. It was a code that Hope had recovered money hidden from an earlier armored car robbery.

But for all of his bravado, Hope apparently got homesick at Christmas. And made a mistake.

The Hunt Moves to Memphis

Moriarty says cost was no object in Texas when it came to hunting fugitives.

"Because their attitude is if you don't catch one, you will be chasing them all. And so we put electronic surveillance on the phones of some known associates, and there was a woman that we suspected that he had had an affair with that was residing in the Dallas area. And on Christmas day, the phone got multiple calls. Her phone, as well as some others that we were looking at, got multiple calls from the Memphis area.

A few days after Christmas, Moriarty and Fawcett headed to Memphis to pursue the new lead. Police in a suburb of Memphis found an abandoned 1985 beige over brown 4-door Oldsmobile 98 with a luggage rack on the rear trunk and mud flaps on the rear tires. It was the vehicle that Hope had carjacked from the elderly man.

Moriarty and Fawcett arrived in Memphis at 3 AM on February 2, 1995.

They found clues that Hope had left in the stolen car, including a receipt for an ID photo purchased at a Memphis shopping mall, a newspaper with ads circled for apartments and rental furniture, a receipt from a motel where he had stayed, and a newspaper ad for a Honda CRX with the owner's name and number scrawled on it in Hope's handwriting.

Hope had bought the Honda on December 16, 1994, for $2,850 cash. He was using it to commute back and forth to Dallas to commit the armed robberies.

Hope had been stopped by local police in the Memphis area twice. Fawcett says the officers were very lucky. "When these two uniformed officers stopped him, he was sizing up which one he was going to shoot. He was trying to determine which one was wearing a vest and which one wasn't. But he talked himself right out of a traffic ticket. He convinced him that he got lost in the wrong neighborhood, and they let him go without a warning ticket or anything."

Hope stayed true to the habits of ex-cons on the run. Moriarty traced the phone number that Hope had used to call a girlfriend on Christmas Eve to the executive office of a meat distributor in Memphis. The executive's secretary had stopped by the office with her sister and her boyfriend to make phone calls. She identified Hope as her sister's boyfriend.

Women Love Outlaws

Hope was boldly phoning a girlfriend back in Texas using a phone provided by his new girlfriend. "He was definitely a womanizer. And the old saying, "Women love outlaws," really applied in his circumstance. He played that cowboy image, and he was a con man, said Moriarty.

Cell phones did not exist then. People used pagers for mobile communications.

Posing as his girlfriend, the investigators texted Hope to set up a meeting at a country western dance club.

Hope had told his new girlfriend in Memphis that he owned a country-western bar back in Dallas. The investigators

99

discovered Hope had bought a black Jaguar with his stolen loot.

When the investigators pulled into the Denim and Diamonds night club, Hope's Jaguar was parked in its lot. They saw the butt of a .45 caliber pistol sticking out from underneath the driver's seat. They disabled the car's battery and flattened its tires to prevent a getaway.

Moriarty and Fawcett went inside the sprawling thirty-one thousand square foot dance hall. They fit right in with the crowd. Moriarty worked undercover, so he looked like a scary ex-con with a beard and long hair.

Fawcett didn't look much different and certainly nothing like a cop.

Moriarty spotted Hope in a white straw cowboy hat standing at a table holding court. He was the center of attention. Moriarty was concerned that when they jumped Hope bouncers would intervene.

Coincidentally, a fight erupted in the bar, and police rushed inside, forewarned that Moriarty and Fawcett were about to make a surprise arrest.

They had calmly moved beside Hope and pounced. "Lew and I jumped on him and put him on the ground, and he just could not believe that two cops from Texas were in Memphis taking his ass to jail," recalled Moriarty.

Fawcett told him Hope, "You're going back to Dallas. Your name is Dennis Hope. You're going back to Dallas with us. And he was shocked. He didn't argue, and he didn't resist. I expected we might have a fight on our hands, but he was not armed."

Nearly nine hours after arriving in Memphis and running down dozens of leads, Moriarty and Fawcett took Hope into custody at 11:45 PM on February 2, 1995.

Hope was carrying more than $6,000 in cash and a pager on him.

Their investigation wasn't over. They obtained a subpoena to get the billing information for the pager. The address led to a boarding house where Hope had rented a room shortly after his arrival in Memphis. Forty minutes after Moriarty and Fawcett arrived, Hope called the landlord from jail.

Hope asked if police were there and claimed it was a front for a robbery. Hope asked the landlord to get $17,000 hidden in a TV box and duffle bag as well as a .45 semi-automatic handgun out of the house.

Moriarty and Fawcett found a treasure trove of evidence that would send Hope to prison for the rest of his life.

"He was commuting from Memphis doing the robberies, doing the surveillance, and taking down those places. We found large amounts of cash and currency that were taken in the robberies. But also, he was getting ready to do more armored car stuff. He was putting together a uniform and ID cards from Brink's. He was cutting and pasting ID cards, and they looked pretty good," recounted Moriarty.

In an unusual twist of fate, Hope's new Memphis girlfriend collected the $5,000 reward for his capture and kept the Jaguar.

Back Behind Bars

Back in custody at the Dallas County Jail, Hope bluntly told me and the FBI that he was planning his next escape.

Jail Commander Bob Knowles was worried. "I don't think I've ever seen anybody that has spent the time to plan as he does, and he is very patient."

When I approached his jail cell, Hope was doing pushups in a handstand position. He would do hundreds of them every day and would run in place for hours. He was already training for his next break to freedom.

A Relentless Desire to Escape

Five officers escorted Hope out of his cell for our interview. They placed him in handcuffs and leg irons. Wearing an orange prison jumpsuit, Hope shuffled his feet to our meeting.

He wore a vest that delivered an electric shock similar to a super stun gun to prevent him from escaping again on the way to court. At the first sign of trouble, guards could press a remote control button that would send a 50,000-volt charge for 8 seconds into Hope's lower back muscles.

I watched a video demonstration of the vest. It knocked burly deputies off their feet into kicking and screaming fits. None of these extra security measures discouraged Hope. Not one bit.

Hope demonstrated on camera how he could twist the plastic ink refill from my ballpoint pen into a handcuff key. His guards watched, stunned, as did the Dallas County Sheriff when he watched my television news report later that evening. The Sheriff immediately banned ballpoint pens.

Leaving Dead or Alive

Hope defiantly told me that he would not stop trying to escape, "I look at it as if they kill me while I am trying to get away, then the state didn't get the 80-year prison sentence of out me."

Making good on his promise, during a federal court appearance, Hope pick-pocketed a guard's handcuff key and swallowed it.

That was the last straw for the Dallas County Sheriff. He wanted Dennis Hope out of his jail.

After angry exchanges, the U.S. Marshals moved Hope to a privately run jail.

Hope wrote a friend, "The facility isn't a year old and is falling apart. Doors stay ajar because the foundation is shifting, and the cell doors can easily be opened." And in closing, he noted. P.S. I am using a ballpoint pen.

A few weeks later, Hope sprung open the remote locking device on his cell door. He assaulted a guard with a metal drain cover he had pried loose from the shower and briefly took over the command center.

Afterward, officers found hacksaw blades and a shank made of a toothbrush. He had almost sawed through a door lock. And he had already been caught trying to dig through a wall.

Then Assistant U.S. Attorney David Finn prosecuted Hope on federal charges.

"He is extremely intelligent. He is extremely wily. Most criminals, particularly violent criminals, are not nearly as intelligent as Mr. Hope, which is really the tragedy here because he could obviously apply himself to something productive."

Stop The Energizer Bunny

On August 18, 1995, a seven-man, five-woman federal jury deliberated for less than an hour before convicting Hope on eight counts of robbery, felony possession of a firearm, and carjacking.

During the four-day trial, the jury was shown my televised interview with Hope.

Federal prosecutor David Finn called Hope cagey, dangerous, and savvy. He urged the jury to put an end to this one-man crime machine. "He is essentially the criminal equivalent of the energizer rabbit. He keeps going and going and going both in prison and outside of prison."

During the trial, U.S. Marshals had to strap Hope to a bare chair. They removed the chair's leather cover to prevent Hope from prying loose upholstery tacks to use as a weapon.

Before the verdict, he scuffled with officers. And threatened to stab his court-appointed attorney in the skull with a pencil.

The judge stacked a 72-year federal prison sentence on top of Hope's 80-year Texas sentence. Hope concluded, "When a man has been sentenced to be locked up the rest of his life, common sense would lead you to believe his intentions."

Inside A Concrete Fortress Named Telford

A year later, Hope was still defiant when I interviewed him inside the supermax Telford Unit in rural northeast Texas.

The Telford Prison unit looks like a massive concrete bunker surrounded by rings of security fences and rolls of razor-sharp concertina wire.

Hope found himself under the scrutiny of Jack Garner, who was then regarded as one of the toughest prison wardens in Texas.

I asked Warden Garner, "What do you do with a Dennis Wayne Hope, who has nothing to lose?" Garner sternly replied, "My opinion is we lock him up right where he is at and throw away the key. Dennis Wayne Hope should never get out of the penitentiary."

A Prison Inside a Prison

The prison system put Hope into Administrative Segregation called Ad-Seg.

It's a prison within a maximum-security prison. John Moriarty, with a grin and tinge of humor, described Hope's restricted life inside solitary confinement. "He is so far back in the penitentiary they are feeding him with a slingshot. You have 23 hours a day single-celled, one hour out to shower and recreate. It's the bowels of the prison. And you're afforded all of the care required by law, but it's the tightest security in the prison system."

I had reported from inside administrative segregation units and noted that inmates receive meals through a locked slot that opens in the door. Moriarty described it.

105

"They call it a bean slot. And that's how you get fed. And when you are taken out of that cell, you back up and put your arms through that hole, and you're handcuffed, and there's a leash put on you, and the doors open, and you know you're in custody."

The first time I entered an Ad-Seg unit, I was overwhelmed by the constant din of yelling by inmates. It felt like I had entered a dog kennel of angry pit bulls. Moriarty agreed with my impression.

"It's a very violent place. It's the place where people who can't act properly in prison, which is saying a lot, are put. The chances of you having feces and urine thrown on you and other liquids that they heat with what they call a stinger for boiling coffee or soup is very likely. It's a dangerous place to work. I mean, it's the worst of the worst."

Dennis Hope's tiny cell contained a small sink built on the top of a seatless toilet made of stainless steel in a prison factory. He slept on a thin cloth mattress atop a steel slab, both of which were also made in a prison factory.

Daylight shined through a small slit in the wall near the ceiling. No one was tall enough to see outside.

Two guards armed with metal batons came to escort Hope to his daily one-hour recreation. Guards used a wrench to open the so-called "bean slot" in his cell door.

They ordered Hope to strip down, lower his boxer shorts and bend over for a visual anal cavity inspection for weapons. The guards told Hope to turn around, place his arms behind his back, and extend his wrists through the slot in the door to get handcuffed.

When the cell door slid open, the guards firmly grasped Hope by each arm and walked him down the cellblock.

Inside a caged recreation yard, I watched Hope perform his daily regimen of physical training, running laps and doing hundreds of handstand-style push-ups.

Warden Garner wasn't the least bit worried that Hope was training for his next escape. The warden beamed with pride that an inmate who had escaped from him to Mexico a decade earlier had just been captured.

The Warden had kept the inmate's photograph in his wallet as a reminder and pledged that Hope would never get away. Garner emphatically stated, "I promise you if Hope ever runs off, I will be on Hope's doorstep every step of the way."

Dennis Hope confidently told me that the old-time wardens like Garner would retire someday, and the prison system would forget about his notorious escapes. Hope would bide his time and plan another break for freedom.

In a 2009 letter to a British television producer interested in his story, Hope stated, "In some areas, I threw caution to the wind. To me, life is defined by more than just a heartbeat, it's about living and enjoying some, if not all of what you do. It would serve no purpose to be on the lam if I were just hiding under a rock. I never had any intentions of coming back to prison. I'd either be dead or exercising my freedom somewhere in the United States."

Hope's defiance seared these televised threats into the administration of the prison system. He quit boasting after spending more than 27 years in solitary confinement, 22 to 24 hours a day, in a cell smaller than the parking space for a compact car.

On February 2022, in pleas to the U.S. Supreme Court, Hope said he suffered from depression and paranoia, feared he was going insane, and thought about killing himself. He asked the high court to consider whether such prolonged isolation violated the Eighth Amendment, which bars cruel and unusual punishment.

Hope wrote to his lawyers that "challenging the use of solitary confinement has given me a purpose and goal and helped me maintain a degree of sanity in an otherwise insane environment."

The U.S. Supreme Court declined to hear Hope's case. But in the wake of his lawsuit, Texas released him from administrative segregation into the prison system's general population, where he had more freedom.

Afterward, Hope's lawyer stated, "he has gotten to shake another human being's hand and to feel the grass under his feet for the first time in more than half of his lifetime."

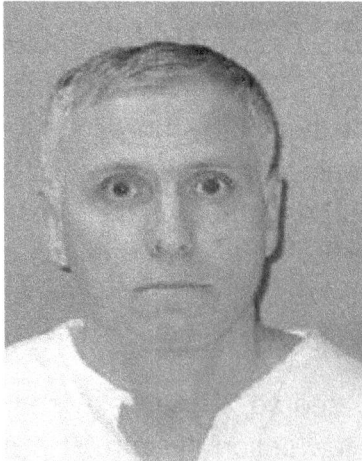

Dennis Wayne Hope TDCJ
Mug Shot 2024

In his 2024 prison mugshot, 55-year-old Hope is pictured with a strong jaw and short salt-and-pepper hair.

The Parole Board has turned down Hope's request for parole 16 times, citing his criminal history for eleven offenses and his conscious disregard for the lives of others, meaning they believe that he poses a continuing threat to public safety.

Will the lure of freedom and the prospect of never getting out prompt Hope to make another prison break?

Three decades ago, his last words to me were, "I've got nothing to lose."

Blood, Witchcraft, and Methamphetamine: The Dark Secrets of the Waco Cult

They were known as the Devil Lovers, a clandestine group of middle-aged men and women from prominent families in Central Texas centered around Waco. Every Wednesday night at exactly 11 PM, they met in an industrial warehouse. Upon arrival, they would shed their clothes and don floor-length satin robes emblazoned with names like Black Warlock and White Witch.

Forming a circle, they would prick their fingers with a needle, allowing three drops of blood to splatter onto the pages of an open Bible. This ritualistic bloodletting was a solemn pledge to respect the order and protect their brothers and sisters. At the helm of this eerie assembly was David Russell Zell, the self-proclaimed master of the circle, distinguished by his robe adorned with a five-star mystical pentagram and the title 'Master' sewn above it.

The Cult of Crank

Artist Depiction Cult of Crank Devil Worshippers

This was no ordinary cult; it was a cult of crank—methamphetamine. These devil worshippers were behind the operation of the largest illicit meth lab in Texas during the late 1980s. Remarkably, except for the meth cook, a man nicknamed 'The Professor,' none of the members were meth users themselves.

David Zell was a somewhat nerdy guy who drifted into Texas from the state of Ohio with a few petty crimes under his belt. He was looking for gullible people to exploit. So, he started frequenting local bars and restaurants, where he began to gather a small but growing group of followers. His charisma drew in a diverse crowd—local business owners, real estate agents, students, and others—all captivated by his talk of the dark side. He preached that real power lay in the dark arts and promised to teach them how to harness it. At first, it wasn't clear if he spelled it out explicitly, but it soon became evident: this was about Satan worship. To spice things up, he threw in a bit of witchcraft for good measure.

Zell's influence grew to the point where he and his followers rented a building near downtown Waco—a significant upgrade from their previous, smaller meeting place. As he became more profitable, their gatherings became more elaborate. They would strip off their clothes, don long satin robes, and listen to Zell's lectures. They drew a large satanic pentagram on the floor and conducted ceremonies, dedicating themselves to him and the dark side.

Shift From Marijuana to Meth

But Zell wasn't just about the rituals. He was lazy and didn't like to work, so he saw an opportunity to make money. Initially, they dabbled in marijuana, but it wasn't profitable enough. Methamphetamine was a different story. What costs $100 a gram—about the size of a Sweet'N Low sweetener package—could sell for tens of thousands of dollars per pound. So, they transitioned from marijuana to meth.

To run this devil-loving organization efficiently, they needed a professional. Enter Roy Wells Junior, one of Texas's best meth cooks at the time. Despite having only an eighth-grade education, Wells, nicknamed 'The Professor,' was a master of large-scale meth production. He had his handwritten formula and specialized in producing large quantities of meth. Wells set up a lab in a massive 12,000-square-foot warehouse with three triple-neck glass flasks like those in a university chemistry lab.

When law enforcement finally caught up with them, they found 61 pounds of meth in solution, ready to be powdered out. That's how large the operation had become in just a few weeks. Wells, despite his lack of formal education, was incredibly clever. He looked like a stereotype of a redneck, but his skills in meth production were unmatched.

A Frightening Operation Unveiled

This was the world of David Zell and his followers—a bizarre blend of satanic rituals and industrial-scale drug manufacturing that would shock even the most seasoned investigators.

Imagine David Zell standing in the dimly lit bars of Waco, Texas, his eyes gleaming with a mix of charisma and cunning. He wasn't preaching your typical Baptist sermon. No, Zell's pitch was something entirely different. It was shocking, provocative, and utterly mesmerizing.

Perhaps for some, the traditional Baptist sermons had lost their allure. Maybe Zell, an outsider, recognized the gullibility of these locals and knew exactly how to exploit it. He presented them with something new, something forbidden. It was the allure of the dark side, wrapped in mystery and power.

At first, his message might have been shocking. But as they listened, these people began to find it intriguing, even appealing. They thought it was cool, rebellious, and a bit naughty. And these weren't impressionable teenagers dabbling with a Ouija board. These were adults, many of them with college degrees and successful careers—business owners, real estate agents, and professionals. Despite their accomplishments, they found themselves drawn to Zell's dark charisma.

Zell's appeal lay in offering them a taste of the forbidden, a break from the mundane. His followers weren't just anyone; they were grown, established individuals who should have known better. Yet, they sold out to him, seduced by the thrill of the unknown and the promise of power.

For reasons unknown, a peculiar group began to coalesce around the enigmatic figure of David Zell. This assembly, which would later become infamous for its methamphetamine production and distribution skills, also had a dark undercurrent of sexual manipulation. Zell, like other cult leaders before him, used sex as a form of control and reward, trading or gifting women within the group. This was eerily reminiscent of other notorious cults where leaders exerted similar control over their followers' personal lives.

The allure of cults lies in their ability to make followers believe that their eternal well-being or fate is tied to the leader's commands. Once this belief takes hold, followers become willing to do anything—be it sexual acts, committing violence, or other heinous deeds—in the name of obedience. And obey they did.

Texas DPS Investigates

In Texas, the State Police, known as the Texas Department of Public Safety (DPS), boasted one of the finest narcotics investigative units in the Southwest during that era. Always on the lookout for meth sources, DPS agents worked closely with informants who would make undercover purchases. One such informant bought meth that was still slightly wet and carried a strong, pungent smell—a telltale sign that the lab was nearby.

Methamphetamine, especially the older phenyl acetic acid-based type, has a distinctive odor, often compared to perfumes. Recognizing this, the agents knew they were closing in on the source. The informant continued making purchases until a local businessman she was buying from became suspicious. He took her hands and suggested lighting a candle, claiming he had someone who could look inside her. Frightened, she escaped and reported, saying she was done with the operation.

With the scent of meth leading them closer, agents began surveilling the group. They observed late-night meetings, followed the members north on Interstate 35, and soon pinpointed a large industrial warehouse as the likely lab location. In those days, the mere smell of meth production was enough to establish probable cause for a search warrant.

The Warehouse Raid

Early one morning, an agent detected the familiar smell and called for immediate action. By 9 AM, a team was ready to raid the warehouse. Just as they arrived, a member of the group was entering the building, closing the large steel garage door behind him. The agents quickly rammed the door to prevent it from shutting completely, allowing them to storm inside.

The scene inside was a testament to the group's preparation for violence. Weapons were everywhere—61 firearms, including eight machine guns, sawed-off shotguns, and other deadly weapons, all loaded and ready to fire. As they breached the door, only one member managed to reach for a gun. In the so-called powdering out room, filled with four five-gallon drums of acetone, a young woman grabbed a .38 pistol. A DEA agent drew his weapon and ordered her to drop it. Had he fired, the spark could have ignited the acetone, causing an explosion that would have destroyed the entire block.

Miraculously, she complied, and the raid proceeded without any fatalities. This operation marked a significant victory in dismantling the meth empire of the Devil Lovers, exposing the dark and dangerous world orchestrated by David Zell.

A Pattern of Paranoia and Arsenals

In my investigations of methamphetamine rings and other criminal groups, one disturbing trend stands out: the proliferation of firearms. This was evident in previous cases, like that of Mr. Z, a Dallas Meth kingpin that I covered who had an arsenal of air-to-ground rockets, grenades, and bazooka rounds—enough firepower to outfit a small army. We saw similar stockpiling with David Koresh, the leader of the Branch Davidian cult at his compound outside Waco, who amassed tens of thousands of rounds and converted weapons to fully automatic. And now, with David Zell and the Devil Lovers, the pattern continued.

So, what drives these groups to accumulate such vast arsenals? Paranoia is a significant factor. They know they're breaking the law and are constantly wary of law enforcement closing in. Zell once confided to a group member, "I think the police are following us. But Satan, he'll protect us, don't worry." Of course, he and Satan were both wrong, but this mindset explains their readiness to engage in a final, desperate showdown with authorities.

After discovering the staggering number of firearms in the Devil Lovers' warehouse—61 in total, including eight machine guns—investigators knew they had to search their residences. The apartments were a mix of normality and chaos. In one, amidst the clutter of everyday life, investigators found a box of magic spells in the kitchen, listing incantations for everything from causing car wrecks to personal protection. It was both absurd and chilling.

Bizarre and Macabre Finds

In another apartment, investigators stumbled upon something even more unsettling. As they entered with the apartment manager, a red light from a closet illuminated a makeshift altar. There was a goat's head, a stone tablet with Satanic symbols, and bones. To the left hung their ceremonial robes—the black robe of the master, the white robe of the white witch, and the red robe of the black warlock. The scene was so bizarre and dark that it spooked the apartment manager, who fled and never returned.

Amid the oddities, investigators found 11 pounds of meth powder worth hundreds of thousands of dollars. They also discovered a drilled hole leading from one closet to another apartment below, indicating further hidden activities. The extent of Zell's influence and the depth of the cult's operations were staggering.

Despite the raids, David Zell was nowhere to be found. He wasn't at the lab, with its bubbling meth and acetone drums, nor in the apartments with the witchcraft paraphernalia. Zell had vanished.

However, luck was on the investigators' side. Within a day, they received a lead: Zell had been arrested and released in

Arizona under a fake name, but his fingerprints matched. Further electronic evidence suggested he might be in Las Vegas.

One Texas Ranger One Fugitive

We needed Zell, the leader, to dismantle the group entirely. Enter Texas Ranger John Aycock, a seasoned fugitive hunter. With his unique aura and relentless pursuit, Aycock was dispatched to track down Zell. His mission: bring the elusive master of the Devil Lovers to justice and end their reign of terror.

Texas Ranger John Aycock boarded a plane bound for Las Vegas, a city known for its quirks and oddities. Las Vegas was a hotbed for fugitives back then, perhaps even more so than Los Angeles. The FBI had a dedicated fugitive squad, leveraging intelligence from casinos staffed by former law enforcement officers. When Aycock arrived, he was met by the FBI.

Without a firearm—standard for a Texas Ranger traveling out of state back then—the FBI agent inquired about his readiness. "John, what are you carrying?" the agent asked. "Well, I'm not carrying a firearm," Aycock replied. The agent, slightly bemused, responded, "Aren't you after a devil worshiper? These guys have guns and are crazy." He then opened the trunk of his car, revealing an arsenal of weapons. "Pick what you want," he offered. Aycock selected a couple of firearms, and they set off on their hunt for David Zell.

Meanwhile, unbeknownst to us at the time, Zell's son was also a wanted man. Having gone AWOL from the Army at Fort Carson, Colorado, he was missing and had a warrant out for his arrest. Aycock and the FBI agent scoured the casinos with photographs in hand. One casino, Circus Circus, reported seeing someone who matched Zell's description.

Fear and Loathing in Vegas

They headed to Circus Circus, and there, playing seven-card stud, was David Zell. Across from Zell, on a slightly elevated platform, sat his son, cheating for him by signaling his opponents' cards. This mini-cheat scheme was about to come to an abrupt end.

With his usual calm demeanor, Aycock sidled up next to Zell and whispered, "I'm John Aycock with the Texas Rangers, and you're under arrest." At that moment, the FBI agent attempted to grab Zell's son, who leaped over the rail to escape. Zell was knocked off his chair, and chaos erupted at the card table.

The arrest disrupted the game, and Zell and his son were taken into custody. Shockingly, Zell confessed to most of the drug activities and many of the bizarre rituals he had been involved in. Why did a guy who leads a satanic group and controls members of the cult with a spell suddenly confess? Ranger Aycock simply replied, "Hell, he was impressed. He said, 'We got out there the same day that Zell arrived in Las Vegas, and the Texas Rangers caught him.' He was impressed. So he confessed."

The Trial and Towering Evidence

David Zell stood trial at the federal courthouse in Waco, Texas. The jury was terrified by the sheer volume of evidence and the dark nature of his crimes.

The fear in the courthouse was palpable. Armed agents were stationed throughout, and the jury was gripped by the constant fear that members of Zell's cult might attempt a breakout.

The federal judge overseeing the case allowed prosecutors to present all the firearms investigators had seized. They stacked them high on a table in the courtroom—a mountain of weapons that rattled and clattered with every addition. By the time the last firearm was placed, they would bounce and roll down the pile, a stark testament to the sheer firepower the Devil Lovers had amassed. Though they were all rendered safe and unloaded, the sight was overwhelming.

The evidence presented at the trial was damning. Chemists and other experts testified to the extent of the drug operation. One of the cult members turned against the rest, providing insider testimony that left no doubt about their guilt. The case was overwhelming, and the jury quickly returned a guilty verdict for all involved.

Despite their decisive action, the jury was understandably shaken. Before leaving the courthouse, they made a special request: could the Marshals escort them to their cars, watch them get in, and ensure they left safely? The sight of the cult's robes and the bizarre, dark evidence had spooked them deeply.

But in the end, their courage shone through. They convicted the cult members, ensuring justice was served, and made it home safely, a testament to their bravery in the face of such unsettling darkness.

A Con Man Unmasked

One of the female cult members testified that David Zell had a peculiar habit of constantly asking his followers, "Do you love me?" It was a strange, almost needy question from a man who wielded such dark influence.

A prosecutor painted a vivid picture of Zell's true nature. "He was just a conman who wanted the good life on easy street," the prosecutor said. "The psychology of David Zell was that he was a phony. He could have been selling vacuums door-to-door as easily as he sold Satan. He was just full of bull."

Zell's motivations were clear: he craved an easy life and a lot of money. By the time they were manufacturing and selling meth, profits were soaring, despite some of the money mysteriously disappearing—likely due to Roy Wells Junior's sticky fingers. Zell, however, had moved on to bigger and better things, securing a house once owned by a former Baylor University football coach. It was a beautiful home in an upscale suburban area, a stark contrast to the grimy world of meth labs and satanic rituals.

Ultimately, Zell's psychology was that of a classic con man. He constantly sought validation, wanting to be liked, loved, and admired. This need for approval was woven into his deceptive personality, driving his actions and manipulations. Zell's story, filled with dark manipulations and a thirst for easy wealth, serves as a chilling reminder of how easily people can be led astray by a charismatic but ultimately hollow figure.

The Professor's Downfall

In a second trial under the federal armed career criminal law, a federal prosecutor brought to justice Roy Lee Wells, the notorious meth cook known as "The Professor." Wells, who had a lengthy rap sheet filled with violent crimes and drug trafficking charges, faced a hefty forty-year prison sentence.

Attempting to escape his fate, Wells appealed the sentence, claiming that his legal counsel had been incompetent. He argued that the testimony about his use of women as sexual gifts and his knowledge of voodoo should never have been allowed in court. However, the appeals court saw through his ploy and rejected his claim.

A Grim Legacy in Federal Custody

As of June 2024, Roy Lee Wells resides in the Bureau of Prison's federal medical center in Springfield, Missouri. Now 70 years old, he awaits his release in 2040, when he will be 86 years old. His story serves as a grim reminder of the dark underbelly of the methamphetamine trade and the lengths to which its key players will go to evade justice.

Nightmare In The Fastlane: The Terminator's Reign of Terror Against Truckers

I try to explore not just the "what" and the "who" but the often elusive "why" behind murders.

This chapter features my interview with mass killer Doug Feldman on Texas Death Row.

The why could not be more elusive or irrational in his case.

Feldman was once a successful college-educated financial analyst, the life of the party after hours.

But he became a short-fused ticking time bomb riding a black Harley Davidson motorcycle.

Feldman pulled alongside a tractor-trailer rig rolling down Central Expressway toward the heart of downtown Dallas at night.

The Terminator

He resembled Arnold Schwarzenegger, the cyborg assassin in the 1984 movie *The Terminator*.

He calmly pointed a 9mm pistol at the truck driver's side window.

Flames erupted from its barrel as five deadly bullets left the gun's chamber.

The truck's 36-year-old driver hung on for life long enough to steer the big rig to the side of the road and stop before hitting other vehicles.

He was pronounced dead on arrival at a hospital emergency room.

Police thought it was a case of road rage until a call came in forty minutes later.

A security camera at a gasoline filling station miles away captured a blurry image of a bearded, long-haired man riding a black Harley motorcycle up to the driver of an Exxon gasoline tanker truck who was unloading fuel.

The motorcycle rider shot the 62-year-old driver to death. He never saw it coming.

In the wake of the shootings, TV news stations played and replayed the security camera footage to try to get the public to identify the killer.

In the preceding weeks, the showroom window of a Volkswagen car dealership located on the same highway had been shot up.

A few days after the truck murders, a Land Rover rolled into the parking lot of a fast-food restaurant.

In broad daylight, its driver randomly shot a man talking on a payphone outside. The 33-year-old victim survived a gunshot wound in his chest and one in his leg.

A witness jotted down the license plate number of the Land Rover and gave the police a description.

Later, Dallas officers trailed the killer to his mother's apartment.

They arrested 40-year-old Doug Feldman with a 9mm pistol lying on the front seat beside him in plain view.

Feldman had shaved off his long hair and beard following news coverage of the earlier shootings.

An Encounter with a Killer on Death Row

I interviewed Doug Feldman on Texas Death Row in November of 1999, shortly after he had been convicted of Capital Murder and sentenced to die by lethal injection in the Texas Death Chamber.

Doug Feldman Interview with Robert Riggs Texas Death Row

His motive for the deadly shootings was beyond my comprehension. Feldman's anger rose as he talked with me eye to eye, "I think I had also become fed up, I become fed up with being a victim with no redress. And I think there was a part of me that just wanted to start addressing things on a direct and immediate basis. Kind of like you screw me, I'm gonna shoot you for it. That's the frame of mind I was in, which is what happened.

Feldman spoke to me from inside a locked wire cage in the Death Row visitation room at the Ellis Prison unit.

He wore a white prison uniform. His black hair was cut short into a burr style. He appeared not to have shaven for a few days. Thick black eyebrows protruded above his blue-gray eyes, which darted from side to side.

They weren't the dead, piercing shark-like eyes that I was accustomed to seeing on the serial killers that I had interviewed here.

But like those killers, there wasn't an ounce of remorse for the strangers that he had randomly killed.

A Boiling Pot of Irrational Anger

An angry, irrational rage boiled inside Feldman.

"I think when you get to the point that I was it's basically war. Basically, I'm declaring war man. If I saw you on the street I might have shot you. I might have shot that guy right there. (pointing to my teenage son who accompanied me). I might have shot this guy right over here(pointing to a guard). Didn't really give a fuck. I feel like I was exceedingly sparing. I had 400 rounds of ammunition; I could have easily done a Benbrook (referring to a church shooting). I could have easily shot 30 or 40 people before they caught me. I shot those two guys. And I got upset, you know, and I knew that was not the answer. So I snapped, you know? I don't know. I can't explain, I can't explain why.

It was at that moment that I realized I had made a mistake.

Feldman had pointed at guards, at me, and at my 16-year-old son as the persons he would like to have killed on the spot that day.

My son had asked to tag along to see what Dad, the reporter, did for a living.

Boy, did he find out.

I had grown so numb to the gruesome, violent stories that I heard from inmates by the dozens inside Texas maximum-security prisons that it did not occur to me that an innocent teenager might not be ready for this.

My son recently confided that it scared him to death. And I think you would have been scared hearing Feldman justify murder.

"That's funny. That's the way society works. I've got a legitimate gripe about the way I'm treated. Yeah. But I'm in here because it's my fault. That's the way society works. It puts you in a situation in which you can't really win or address the problem. But if you do something about it, take action or whatever, then you're the criminal. So it's my fault. Okay. I told you there were gonna be some parts that were never going to make sense to you.

The Beast Inside

On his resume, Feldman didn't fit the profile of a mass killer. He had received a Bachelor of Business degree from the upscale Southern Methodist University in Dallas.

He had been a financial analyst for a health care management company – a workaholic – a financial wizard with spreadsheets. A coworker said Feldman was one of the funniest people he had ever met.

His wife had divorced him four years earlier. After the shootings, she said their two-year-long marriage had ended amicably. She remembered Feldman as a wonderful person. "We just weren't a match," she said.

Feldman took the divorce hard. He moved into an apartment where his cocaine-fueled parties established his reputation as a free-wheeling lady's man.

Suddenly, he quit work and went off to South America.

But friends said Feldman did not return the same.

Fueling His Rampage

Once a penny pincher, Feldman bought a $19,000 Harley motorcycle and a Land Rover. He dropped out of society and went into a jealous rage.

"It seemed like life was too difficult. It was too hard earning money, and too many people were working against me, you know, in legitimate business interests. I don't know, life just seemed unfair. You know, I would see things on the news where people like JFK Jr. just had millions fall into their lap because their great-grandfather was some kind of robber baron, you know, 100 years ago. And so this guy grew up and went to fucking Yale and, or Harvard or wherever he went and has an airplane and flies out to fucking Nantucket. And you know, has a condo in New York and one in San Francisco and one in Singapore or wherever, you know, he has a boat. It's like shit. You know, I'm sitting here working my ass off, trying to stay out of trouble. You know, trying to do things the right way. And this guy just has some sort of Cinderella life. And at some very basic level, that really pissed me off because I worked hard. I mean, I worked hard. I made almost straight A's at SMU."

I reminded Feldman that life is not always fair, which provoked another angry response.

"Bullshit. Well, maybe percentage-wise, you're probably right. I don't know, what about these 20-year-old kids who have a dot com? I saw some in the paper the other day, some 20-year-old kid started some.com. And now he has a fucking $3 million house in Sausalito, north of San Francisco. And he's sitting in, I saw pictures of his room. He's got glass walls that look out over the floors. And I'm thinking what 20-year-old kid deserves to have $100 million? I don't know. I was angry that everything that I had to try to accomplish seemed to be so difficult. While for other people it fell into their lap. And maybe that was my own mentality, my own fault. I mean, I know we're getting off-topic."

Feldman complained that he had played the corporate game. He enrolled in one of the best universities, as society expected. Feldman said he should have opted for a laid-back lifestyle running a beach fishing business. He admitted that as he grew older he became more paranoid that he would not find money and a stable life.

After the slayings of the two truck drivers, detectives began running down the owners of black Harley motorcycles.

A Chilling Revelation

They came knocking at the door of Feldman's apartment.

Those detectives don't know how lucky they were that day.

Feldman told me, "I wasn't ready to die. But I was damn sure angry enough to kill somebody else. I almost shot those two detectives that day on my porch. They weren't wearing any body armor. And they were asking me a bunch of questions. And they came up there wearing their guns. You know, it was like they were looking for trouble."

Little did the detectives know that Feldman had a high-powered handgun in his hand concealed by the door jamb. He chuckled that if he were a cop looking for a murder suspect, he would have worn body armor. Feldman had looked the detectives up and down to determine that neither wore a bullet-resistant vest.

While awaiting trial, Feldman wrote in one of 81 letters to a former girlfriend, "I have come to hate every single person on this planet with all my heart and soul. If I had a button that would kill every single person on this planet, I would push it with no hesitation whatsoever!"

The Capital Murder Trial and Feldman's Fury

The jury found Feldman guilty of Capital Murder after deliberating for 20 minutes. During the trial, Feldman repeatedly interrupted testimony hurling profanities at the witnesses.

He had been a ticking time bomb. The jury heard a long list of Feldman's earlier altercations.

When he had been asked to move the door of his Mercedes away from the side of a woman's car, he slammed the door into her car. And sped away laughing.

When Feldman rear-ended another motorist with his Land Rover, he jumped out with a ball peen hammer in hand and smashed the car's hood, windshield, and the driver-side window.

Acceptance of Death

During our interview in November of 1999, Feldman said he looked forward to his date with the executioner. "Some days, I think it'd be nice just to shut my eyes and go to sleep and not have to listen to anybody's bullshit anymore. Not to listen to your voice. Or listen to somebody make a noise, you know. I don't really want to die (laughs), but I'm not totally, you know, against it either.

Feldman's Final Words

Fifteen years later. executions strapped Feldman to a gurney in the Texas death chamber. As lethal chemicals were about to flow into his arm, 55-year-old Douglas Feldman made his last statement with his victim's families looking on from behind one-way glass.

He declared the truck drivers that he had murdered were guilty of crimes that they had committed against him.

"I hereby sentence both of them to death, which I carried out in August of 1998. As of that time, the state of Texas has been holding me illegally in confinement and by force for 15 years. I hereby protest my pending execution and demand immediate relief," he said.

Feldman was pronounced dead 14 minutes later.

Love and Bullets: The True Saga of Bonnie and Clyde

Few stories in the annals of American crime are as compelling and complex as Bonnie Parker and Clyde Barrow's.

They embarked on a notorious bank robbery spree across the central United States during the Great Depression.

Bonnie Parker and Clyde Barron playing to the camera

Their tale interweaves love, violence, and tragedy against a backdrop of economic turmoil.

They became folk heroes to the downtrodden of that era.

Now, portrayed as glamorous outlaws in popular culture, the reality of their lives was far more stark, marked by a relentless pursuit by law enforcement.

I peel back the layers of myth to reveal the human dimension of their infamous journey.

A Prophetic Poem

You've read the story of Jesse James

Of how he lived and died:

If you're still in need

Of something to read

Here's the story of Bonnie and Clyde

That's the first stanza of verses that ran in Dallas' *Daily Times Herald* on the day that Bonnie and Clyde were killed on May 23, 1934, near Gibsland, Louisiana.

The newspaper said it received the verses from Bonnie Parker several months before with the stipulation that it would run only after their deaths.

Bonnie Parker penned that a showdown was coming.

A newsboy once said to his buddy:

I wish old Clyde would get jumped;

In these awful hard times

We'd make a few dimes

If five or six cops would get bumped.

A Public Farewell for the Infamous Outlaw Lovers

Clyde Barrow's remains rested inside the Sparkman-Holz Brand funeral home in downtown Dallas.

More than ten thousand people shouted and demanded to see Clyde Barrow's open casket.

The ornate building's two-story brick neoclassical architectural design featured a monumental pedimented portico of six Corinthian columns.

It had been built for A H Belo after the Civil War. Belo was a Colonel in the Confederate Army and founded the *Dallas Morning News*.

Until 2021, it was known as the Belo Mansion and housed the Dallas Bar Association.

The bar renamed it the Arts District Mansion due to the namesake's ties to the Confederacy.

At the site of Clyde Barrow's funeral in May 1934, a rambunctious crowd pulled up flowers and shrubs by the roots and tossed them into the air.

When police couldn't control the crowd, his family relented and let them inside.

Hundreds of onlookers pushed their way through to see Clyde's body dressed in a light gray suit.

Some exclaimed that they were glad that the 25-year-old gangster was dead.

So, the family shut the funeral home's doors. The crowd left scuffed, dirty floors littered with cigarette butts. Carpets had been pulled up and left in a pile.

Crowd outside Bonnie Parker's funeral May 1934

Across town at the McKamy-Campbell funeral home, a similar scene unfolded. Twenty thousand people pressed to get a peek at Bonnie Parker's body, which was dressed in a silky blue dress.

The throngs crushed the lawn and plowed through a fence.

When the doors opened, five thousand people an hour rambled through, leaving fine carpets destroyed in their wake.

Fifty thousand people viewed the outlaw lovers–that was one-fourth of the population of Dallas in 1934.

A Glamorous and Deadly Image

Bonnie and Clyde's two-year crime spree of robberies and murders across Texas and other states during the Great Depression captivated national attention, embarrassed law enforcement, and terrified communities where they struck.

The outlaw couple competed for headlines with the Depression-era gangsters John Dillinger, Baby Face Nelson, and Pretty Boy Floyd.

It was tough times in America. Four out of ten people were out of work.

Bonnie and Clyde cut a glamorous image. It was seared into public consciousness when a roll of film left in the gang's camera was discovered.

Lawmen surprised them during a deadly shootout in Joplin, Missouri, on April Fool's Day of 1933

The gang barely got away.

Police found a purse with a camera inside that the gang used to photograph themselves.

Press labels Bonnie Parker "Cigar Smoking Gun Moll"

Twenty-two-year-old Bonnie Parker posed with a revolver in her right hand, her left foot on the bumper of a Model A Ford, her left forearm draped over the car's headlight, chomping a cigar sticking out the right side of her mouth.

Bonnie, who weighed less than ninety-nine pounds, wore a slim dress in the fashionable straight flapper silhouette of the time–a dress with broad shoulders and a small waist. She topped it off with a beret and a short modern hairstyle with finger curls tucked beneath it.

Another black and white photograph depicted Bonnie wearing the same outfit, holding a shotgun pressed toward Clyde Barrow as she lifted a handgun from his belt.

Clyde smiled slightly and wore a suit and tie with a fedora tilted back on his head.

Officers on their trail found receipts left behind. One for a green Angora wool dress with a small scarf and matching green belt that cost six dollars and ninety-five cents, equivalent to $152.62 in 2024.

The clothes left the impression among the Depression-ravaged population that crime did indeed pay.

A Life on the Run

But it was not the romanticized story celebrated in the 1967 blockbuster movie *Bonnie and Clyde*.

Living on the run was costly. They often slept in their stolen cars. Injured and hungry. Food came from cans or takeout sandwiches purchased at roadside cafes.

Their families would later say their world had become a 'living hell."

Their crimes attracted national attention and spotlighted the Bureau of Investigation led by J. Edgar Hoover. It raised Hoover's profile to expand from identifying fingerprints and tracking stolen cars that crossed state lines. Hoover turned the bureau into the FBI to take on a greater role in investigating crimes.

Humble Beginnings and a Predestined Path

Bonne Parker, a petite blue-eyed blonde with smiling red lips, showed a knack for writing and a flair for drama in school. She told her sister that her name would end up in lights on Broadway.

But there were few opportunities for girls from poverty-stricken West Dallas near the sewage-filled Trinity River bottoms. It was a place where people didn't lock their doors because there was nothing to steal.

Bonnie Parker married a week before her sixteenth birthday in 1926. On her upper right thigh, she tattooed their names inside hearts.

After less than a year of a troubled marriage, her husband was sent to the state penitentiary, never to be seen by her again.

A Doomed Romance Begins

Three years later, she met Clyde Barrow.

Clyde's family ran a ramshackle gasoline filling station in poverty-stricken West Dallas.

A wood drive-through carport with two hand pumps featured a large advertising sign on its roof for Drink Coca-Cola.

Clyde had a reputation as a car thief, so much so that the Dallas police counted him among their "usual" suspects.

Whenever a car was stolen or a house burglarized, Clyde made the trip downtown to police headquarters.

His mother said that he got picked up by the police so many times at work that he couldn't hold a job and hated the law.

Clyde met Bonnie in 1930 at her brother and sister-in-law's house in West Dallas.

The two were immediately attracted to each other. Bonnie's sister found him charming, laughing and joking, with his dark wavy hair, dancing brown eyes, and dimples that popped out whenever he smiled.

Shortly after they met, the police came to arrest him. Bonnie went crazy, held on to Clyde, and begged the officers to leave him alone.

A couple of months before he had met Bonnie, Clyde, his brother Buck, and a friend had stolen a car, burglarized a home, and stolen a safe. Their crimes had caught up with them.

While awaiting trial behind bars, Bonnie wrote long, dramatic love letters to Clyde. In one letter, she wrote, "I was so blue and mad and discouraged, I just had to cry. I had on Maybelline eyeliner, and it began to stream down my face. I put my head down on the steering wheel and sure did cry."

Clyde pleaded guilty in Waco, Texas, to stealing cars and burglarizing a business. Newspapers dubbed him the "schoolboy" for his baby face appearance and slicked-back hair parted down the middle.

But Clyde was not one to be confined behind bars.

During a jail visit, Bonnie slipped a gun hidden in her bra past guards. Clyde and two cellmates used it to break out of the jail.

A week later, they were caught a thousand miles away during an Ohio crime spree driving a stolen car.

They had forgotten to change the license plates. A Waco newspaper reported their arrest on the front page headlined, "Baby Thugs Captured."

A Brutal Introduction to Prison Life

The judge sentenced Clyde to fourteen years in the Texas penitentiary. He was sent to the Eastham Prison Farm, where guards handed out severe beatings for disobedience.

Guards used a "bat," a two-and-a-half-inch wide, two-foot-long leather strap that was oiled and used to whip the bare backs and buttocks of inmates who misbehaved. The state allowed up to twenty lashings.

The prison's warden defended its use to legislators, saying, "It's just like using spurs on an old horse. When you've got your spurs on, the old horse will do the job."

On the bus ride to prison, Clyde met Ralph Fults, an Eastham escapee who was being returned to prison. Fults warned him that guards would kill inmates for two things: escaping and not working fast enough.

Later, Clyde made his presence known when three guards started beating Fults with the butt of a pistol. With Clyde as a witness, the beating stopped.

Clyde Barrow swore that he would get revenge once he got out.

He got his share of beatings for not keeping up in the prison farm's fields. Inmates called building tenders and trustees would inflict abuse on behalf of the administration in exchange for favorable treatment.

A vicious building tender singled out Barrow for beatings and sexual assaults, according to Fults. Clyde and another inmate were suspected of taking revenge by stabbing the abusive inmate building tender to death.

Hard time inside Eastham got to Clyde. He persuaded a fellow inmate to cut off two toes on his left foot with a sharp tool so he could get transferred to the Huntsville Prison Hospital.

After a few weeks, he received parole and hobbled out of prison on crutches.

Ralph Fults, the escapee that Clyde met on the prison bus and later saved from a beating, said prison changed the youngster who had entered two years earlier from "a schoolboy to a rattlesnake."

Without his two biggest left toes, Clyde would always walk limply.

An Evolution into Armed Robbery

Back in West Dallas, he reunited with Bonnie Parker.

Clyde, Ralph Fults, and another West Dallas ex-con returned to doing what they knew best and had learned from career criminals behind bars—robbing banks.

Clyde Barrow favored the Browing automatic rifle, a weapon from World War I that would spew out twenty bullets in seconds with one pull of its trigger. The gang outgunned law enforcement by arming itself with weapons they stole from National Guard armories.

A Ruthless War on Law Enforcement

Depression-era police were understaffed, underpaid, and poorly trained. By the early nineteen thirties, the Dallas police force had dropped to 255 officers. They didn't have the resources to stake out or tail a suspect. Modern technology and communications equipment did not exist.

Clyde preferred stealing new, fast Ford V-8s with their powerful eight-cylinder engines. In the midst of one of his bloodiest months of killings, Henry Ford received a letter praising the V-8 signed "Clyde Champion Barrow."

Although the handwriting was never authenticated, the Henry Ford Museum holds the letter in its collection.

After Clyde released a kidnapped mail carrier, he was celebrated for his softheartedness among people looking for folk heroes in the depths of the Depression.

With Bonnie in tow, Clyde took her to Eastham prison to inform an inmate that they planned to break him out.

However, Bonnie and Fults were arrested for car thefts in Kaufman, located east of Dallas.

While they were behind bars, Clyde and an accomplice started a robbery spree and murdered a 61-year-old business owner in Hillsboro, Texas. The Texas governor posted a $250 reward.

After Bonnie's release from jail in June 1932, the violence escalated.

Over the next eleven months, Bonnie and Clyde's gang are believed to be responsible for the murder of at least nine law enforcement officers.

Clyde Champion Barron 1933 Wanted Poster

A 1913 memo by the United States Bureau of Investigation, the predecessor to the FBI, noted that "Bonnie Parker is a gun-woman, and it was she probably who shot and killed the Fort Worth Deputy Sheriff" in January.

Mid-1933 proved to be a fatal turning point for the gang. Bonnie was severely injured when Clyde crashed at breakneck speed in the dark. Battery acid splattered on her leg, badly burning it around and below the knee. Her painful wounds never properly heal.

Thirty-year-old Buck, Clyde's brother, was shot in the head when a posse in Iowa converged on them. Buck died in a coma. His wife Blanche was wounded in her left eye by flying glass.

147

In the wake of the callous killings, Dallas police and sheriff's deputies circled the Barrow family filling station four times a day.

Life-size cutouts of Bonnie and Clyde stood in the hall of Dallas police headquarters so officers would know what they looked like.

The run of increasingly violent crimes was approaching an end.

A Vow for Vengeance

In January 1934, Bonnie and Clyde, with two accomplices, returned to the Eastham Prison Farm to break out a member of the gang.

They hid two pistols and ammunition inside a rubber inner tube on prison property. Two inmates recovered the pistols while chopping and stacking wood beneath a heavy fog.

They shot two guards called "high riders" mounted on horses to prevent an escape.

Clyde sped away with the escapees. The prison break made national news. The *New York Times* called it "perfectly executed, aided by the "two-gun, cigar-smoking woman Bonnie Parker, now twenty-three years old, who pounded on the car horn."

Thirty-three-year-old prison guard Major Joseph Crowson died of a gunshot wound to his stomach.

The murder outraged Texas prison director Lee Simmons. He wanted vengeance for the Eastham breakout and Crowson's death.

On February first of nineteen thirty-four, he hired the legendary former Texas Ranger Frank Hamer to track down Bonnie and Clyde.

Just shy of his fiftieth birthday, Hamer had been in more than fifty gunfights and had been called on to control riots and fight the Ku Klux Klan.

Hamer covered more than thirteen hundred miles over the course of a month, studying Bonnie and Clyde's movements.

On April first of nineteen thirty-four, the cold-blooded murder of two motorcycle officers in Grapevine, Texas, today a sprawling community located on the north side of DFW International Airport, drew an extreme rebuke from the press. "Where was the Governor? Where were the Rangers?" asked the *Dallas Dispatch*, which called the Barrow gang "more merciless than rattlesnakes."

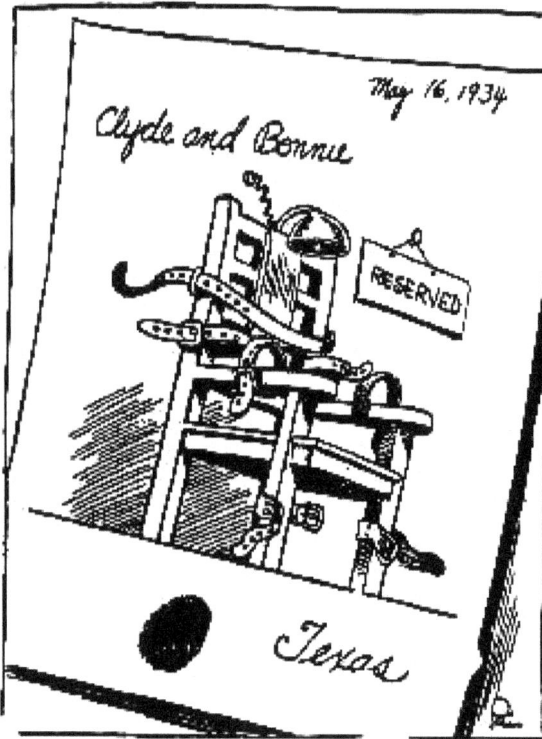

Editorial Cartoon Calls For Bonnie & Clyde To Get The Electric Chair

A witness believed that Bonnie Parker turned over one of the wounded officers and shot him point blank in the chest. Police reported that a cigar stub was found indented with small teeth marks.

Henry Methvin, an Eastham Prison escapee from Louisiana, participated in the brutal, unprovoked shooting.

In a shootout a week later with police in northeastern Oklahoma, a constable was killed, and a wounded officer taken hostage was later released. He believed Bonnie fired a shotgun during the deadly shootout. Bonnie told him that she was offended by news accounts that she smoked cigars.

The Trap is Set

Meanwhile, Henry Methvin's parents cooperated with Ranger Hamer to tip off the fugitive hunters when Bonnie and Clyde were headed to Louisana to meet Henry.

Six officers armed with shotguns, automatic rifles, and pistols set up an ambush.

Henry's father pretended his truck had broken down with a flat tire. Clyde slowed down when he saw him.

Bullet-Riddled 1932 Ford Coupe
Containing the Bodies of Bonnie and Clyde

One of the officers thought Clyde was about to drive off and fired two shots. One hit Clyde in front of his left ear, likely killing him instantly.

Bonnie screamed. "Like a panther," Hamer said later.

A volley of gunfire erupted from the lawmen for several minutes.

After the smoke cleared, bits of blood and tissue splattered the interior of the car.

Part of Clyde's skull had been blown off. Part of Bonnie's right hand was missing.

The car was riddled with bullet holes.

Officer's Inspect impounded "death car" in Dallas.

Officers found automatic rifles, shotguns, pistols, and a thousand rounds of ammunition inside it. Suitcases of clothing, a makeup case, magazines, fifteen license plates, and Clyde's saxophone surrounded the lifeless bodies.

A Legacy in Crime and Culture

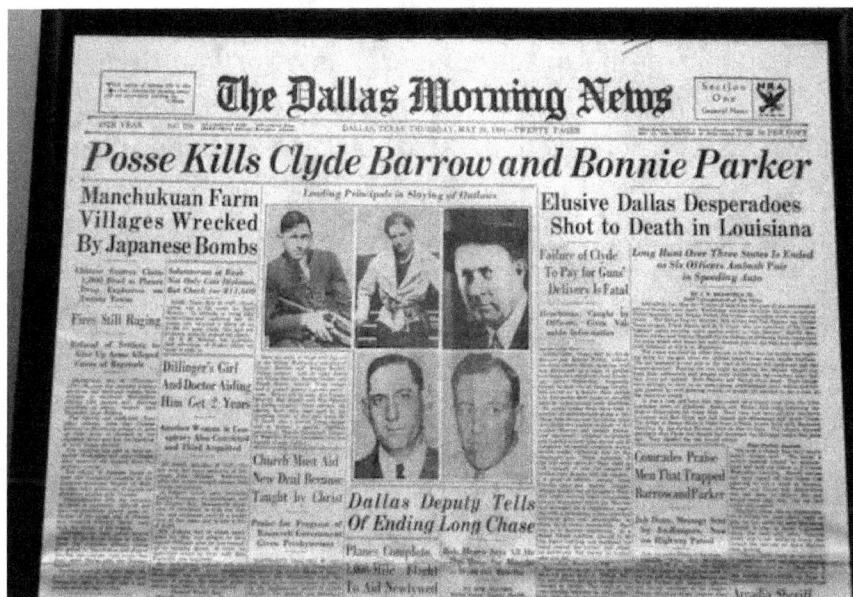

My late mother recalled seeing the bullet-scarred 1934 Ford Model forty B Fordor Deluxe Sedan known as the Bonnie and Clyde "death car" on display at the State Fair of Texas when she was a little girl. She said it was surrounded by crowds who, in a hushed silence, studied the more than 100 bullet holes in the car.

The car is now on display at Whiskey Pete's Hotel and Casino in Primm, Nevada, where it was reportedly purchased for two hundred fifty thousand dollars.

The number of civilians killed by Bonnie and Clyde's gang is a matter of some debate and varies depending on different sources.

It is believed that they were responsible for the deaths of at least thirteen civilians during their crime spree, including store clerks, gas station attendants, and innocent bystanders.

Some sources suggest that the number could be higher, but there is no definitive answer.

Regardless of the exact number, it is clear that Bonnie and Clyde's criminal activities were violent and dangerous, and they posed a significant threat to public safety during their time as outlaws.

At the end of January 1935, twenty-three people with ties to Bonnie and Clyde and their gang members were charged with harboring or assisting criminals, including their mothers.

The two killers who shot prison guard Crowson during their escape from the Eastham Prison Farm were executed in the Texas electric chair known as "Old Sparky" shortly after midnight on May 10, 1935.

A Posthumous Fame

Bonnie Parker penned this closing stanza of the verses she sent to a newspaper before their deaths.

Some day they'll go down together;

They'll bury them side by side:

To few it'll be grief–

To the law a relief–

But it's death for Bonnie and Clyde.

Bonnie's burial wish did not come true.

Her mother, Emma Parker, wanted no such thing.

She said, "Clyde had her for two years. Look what he did to her. Now she's mine. Nobody else has a right to her."

A Dallas writer summed up or fascination with the outlaw couple by writing,

"Romanticized or vilified, criticized or admired, Bonnie and Clyde remain legendary – no longer for who they were, but for who we want them to be."

Death Row Escape into Darkness

On a chilly November night in 1998, Texas witnessed an escape from Death Row that would etch itself into the state's criminal history.

Convicted killer Martin Gurule, defying the odds stacked against any prisoner within such a high-security facility, managed to breach the layers of security to taste freedom.

The last time that happened was in 1934 when Bonnie and Clyde broke a member of their gang out of Texas Death Row in a hail of deadly machine gun fire.

Texas's Death Penalty Legacy

The death penalty in Texas dates back to 1819 when hanging by the neck until dead was the method of execution by individual counties until 1923.

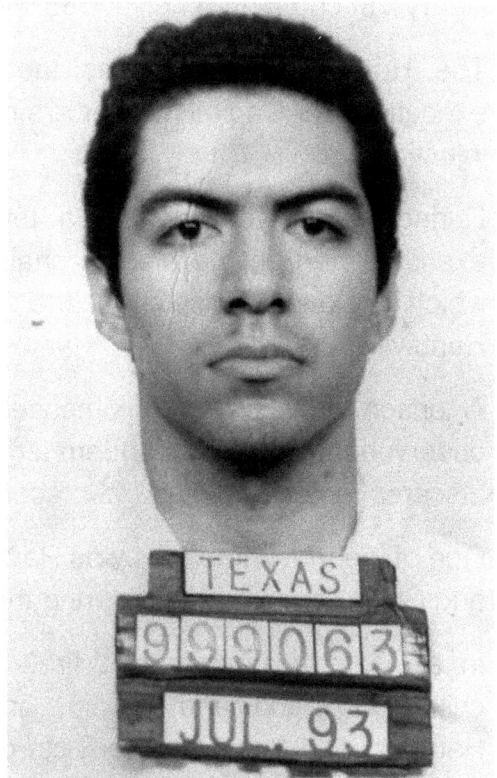

Condemned killer Martin Gurule

Then, state lawmakers authorized using the electric chair, which became known as "old sparky."

The electrocutions were ordered to be carried out in Huntsville, Texas, at the Walls Unit.

Opened in 1849, it is the oldest prison in Texas. Massive red brick walls surround the 55-acre prison in downtown Huntsville. Guards in grey uniforms, armed with rifles, stand watch in sentry towers at each corner of the prison's walls.

It is everything you would imagine a prison to look like. Ominous. Medieval. A bit like the Tower of London, where Henry VIII chopped off his wives' heads.

The Huntsville Unit houses the Death Chamber, where executions for Capital Murder are now administered by lethal injection.

During a forty-year period, a total of 361 inmates were executed here in the electric chair known as "Old Sparky," which is now on display at the Texas Prison Museum in Huntsville.

A prison chaplain who witnessed fourteen electrocutions observed that once the condemned men were strapped down, a scared look came over their faces.

One of the most notorious was Raymond Hamilton, a "Bonnie and Clyde" gang member during the 1930s.

In a blaze of machine-gun fire, Clyde Barrow, Hamilton's childhood friend and cousin, and Bonnie Parker broke Hamilton and four other convicts out of the Eastham prison farm in 1934.

Two prison guards were killed during the escape.

Robert Riggs

The prison break prompted the system's chief to issue a shoot-to-kill order against Bonnie and Clyde.

A prison official hired legendary ex-Texas Ranger Captain Frank Hamer, to hunt down the gangsters.

Hamer, now a Texas Ranger legend, had been in dozens of gunfights and killed at least 53 people,

The portrayal of Hamer in the classic 1967 hit film *Bonnie and Clyde* as a bumbling idiot who gets captured by the pair is inaccurate.

Hamer's widow sued Warner Brothers for defamation, and the studio settled out of court.

Hamer and Louisana officers shot Bonnie and Clyde to death in an ambush on May 23, 1934.

A month later, a prisoner at the Walls Unit smuggled a gun into Clydes' cousin, Raymond Hamilton.

He and two other inmates escaped but were soon recaptured.

Hamilton died a year later in the Texas electric chair.

The last Texas execution using the electric chair occurred in 1964.

"Old Sparky" is now on display at the Texas Prison Museum in Huntsville, drawing curious crowds.

After the Supreme Court struck down the death penalty as cruel and usual punishment, Texas adopted lethal injection in 1977 and conducted its first execution using it in 1982.

Ellis Prison Unit and the Rise of Death Row

Between 1965 and 1999, killers convicted of Capital Murder were held on Texas Death Row at the maximum-security Ellis Prison Unit.

Built in 1963, located ten miles north of Huntsville, the eleven thousand acre prison farm also held more than two thousand other inmates.

Back then, inmates grew cotton, picked it, milled it, spun it, and wove it into enough prison uniforms to clothe a small town of 45 thousand people.

Inmates also raised cows, egg-laying hens, crops, security horses, bloodhounds, and pigs to make the prison system somewhat self-sufficient.

Death Row Garment Factory

I first reported from the Ellis Unit in November 1993 in a series of stories about Texas' prison industries.

Reporter Robert Riggs on Ellis Prison Death Row Guard Tower 1992

The Ellis Unit was surrounded by two twelve-foot-tall fences spaced eight feet apart, topped with large coils of razor-sharp concertina wire.

I went there to report on the Death Row Garment factory.

113 condemned killers made 300 pairs of pants for guards' uniforms daily.

It was the most productive of Texas' thirty-four prison factories.

When I went inside, it was unsettling to discover that some of Texas' most notorious killers used scissors and razor blades to cut cloth.

One of them, Ricky Lee Green of Fort Worth, caught my eye. Three years earlier, I had covered Green's capital murder trial.

Green stabbed a topless dancer 17 times and mutilated her breasts.

During two separate murders of men, Green stabbed and castrated them.

When our eyes met, Ricky Lee Green held a razor blade in one hand as he sliced patterns out of whole cloth.

A death row inmate noticed my shocked expression.

He tried to reassure me that there was a daily count of the razor blades and scissors. "We've never lost a pair," he proclaimed. "We're not monsters out here. I would rather be around these people right here," he said, motioning to the death row inmates working around him, "than be around most of the people out in the free world these days and times."

I wasn't convinced. Most of the violent, hardened inmates that I met were always scheming.

Cold-Blooded Killer Martin Gurule Arrives

Shortly after my news report from Death Row, 23-year-old Martin Gurule arrived.

The five foot, 7 inches tall, 150-pound Hispanic male had thick black hair, a pencil-thin mustache, and brown piercing eyes.

Gurule was a 23-year-old convicted bank robber with a high IQ.

He was sentenced to death in 1993 for murdering the owner of the popular U&I Greek diner in Corpus Christi, Texas, during an armed robbery.

His girlfriend, 23-year-old Malisa Smith, a divorcee and high school dropout, had briefly worked at the restaurant before being fired.

That's when the count of her cash registered drawer was short $350.

Smith returned to the diner after hours with Gurule. She parked outside and watched for police as he held it up at gunpoint.

Gurule cut the phone lines and forced the 46-year-old owner and a 31-year-old cook into a backroom.

He stole $9,000 from the safe, then shot both men execution-style with a bullet to the back of their heads.

Less than a week later, police found the murder weapon, a 10mm Colt Delta Elite semi-automatic pistol, in a room at the home where Gurule lived with his 72-year-old grandmother.

Ballistic tests showed that a bullet and two shell casings found at the restaurant had been fired from the gun, as had a bullet recovered from the slain cook's body.

At his capital murder trial, Gurule insisted on taking the stand to testify in his defense.

Throughout the trial, he acted happy and casual.

On the stand, Garule spun a wild story that the killings were accidental, but the jury didn't buy it.

Afterward, his defense attorney conceded that the physical and circumstantial evidence against Gurule was overwhelming.

A few months later, his 23-year-old girlfriend, Malisa Smith, stood trial for murder.

When police searched her apartment after the robbery, they found bundles of cash hidden in a sombrero hanging on the wall, plus $700 in recently purchased merchandise with the price tags still attached.

Her four-year-old daughter interrupted the murder trial, crying out to her mother from the courtroom gallery.

Prosecutors complained that it was a calculated emotional plea to sway the jury.

The jury convicted Smith of murder and sentenced her to 25 years in prison for her part in the crime.

Meanwhile, when Gurule arrived on Death Row at the Ellis Unit, he was locked inside his cell for 23 hours each day.

He was allowed out only to shower and exercise and was always escorted in handcuffs and leg shackles by guards.

But a few years later, Gurule was granted "work privilege" for good behavior and was allowed to work in the air-conditioned death row garment factory.

Gurule could walk without supervision around cellblock H-17, coming and going between his cell, the dayroom where inmates watched TV, and the fenced-in recreation yard as he pleased.

He learned from a convicted murderer in a neighboring cell how he had used a hacksaw blade to cut through the prison recreation yard chain link fence to try to escape. But he had been caught.

In 1997, an appeals court denied Gurule's motion for a new trial. He wrote to a fellow inmate, "Nobody gets strapped down and lives to tell it. As far as one gets is the death house. I've not yet received a date for execution . . . but I have been affirmed, and I can tell you of one emotion that comes strongly to mind. Desperation."

Thanksgiving Breakout

Shortly after Thanksgiving dinner on the evening of November 26, 1998, the 29-year-old Gurule and six other convicted killers staged their escape from the Ellis I Unit that held 454 death row inmates.

They used black felt tip markers to dye their white prison-issued long underwear black.

The condemned prisoners stuffed their beds with makeshift dummies after Thanksgiving Dinner.

The dummies fooled guards for hours. Even though a count was supposed to occur every 30 minutes, the escape went undetected.

The prison was working on a skeleton staff due to the holiday.

At about 8:15 PM, Gurule and his fellow escapees strolled into the recreation yard about half the size of a basketball court.

Chain-link fencing covered its top and sides.

The yard was located next to their three-story tall cell block – one of three that housed death row convicts.

They used a hacksaw blade to cut a hole into a corner at the top of the chain-link enclosure.

They squeezed through the hole and leaped onto the prison roof, which was flat and partially obscured by a low retaining wall along its perimeter.

Under cover of the night, they made their way on foot a quarter-mile in distance across the rooftops of the prison units to a one-story prison chapel.

Fog rolled in, reducing the visibility of guards watching from six towers.

At a quarter past midnight, the prisoners slid down the chapel's sloped roof to the ground.

The Run to Escape

Gurule, followed by the six other death row inmates, sprinted 75 yards to the perimeter fences at the midway point between two guard towers.

The inmates had wrapped their torsos and legs with cardboard and bundles of magazines to protect them from getting cut or tangled up in the coils of concertina razor wire mounted at the top of the fence.

Eighteen rifle shots rang out. Six of the inmates dropped to the ground. They gave up.

The wiry Gurule scaled the outside fence. He dropped to the ground and ran.

The guards found blood there and thought they might have wounded him.

Gurule disappeared into a heavy morning fog and headed toward a swamp.

More than 500 law enforcement officers launched a massive manhunt for the fugitive.

Two helicopters circled for miles around the prison.

Officers put up roadblocks and conducted door-to-door searches of neighboring farmhouses.

Escapees Rap Sheet

Embarrassed prison officials could not explain how so many high-risk convicted killers went missing undetected for so long.

Here's a rundown of the capital murder convictions of Gurule's six accomplices.

- Kidnap and murder of a Houston woman.
- Kidnap and murder of an elementary school teacher. Her body was found wrapped in a blanket off the side of a rural road. Her hands and ankles were bound with

a telephone cord, and she had been shot in the head, neck, and shoulder with a rifle.

- Kidnap and murder of a man who was singled out because he was gay and shot nine times.
- Robbery and shotgun murder of a clerk at a beverage warehouse.
- Hired as a hitman by a former police officer to kill the officer's wife.
- Robbery and murder of a Houston jewelry store owner.

The escapees had planned to flee to sunny Florida, robbing banks along the way.

An Embarrassing Security Breach

One of the six murderers had tried to escape from death row a few years earlier using a hacksaw blade.

A death row guard revealed that every recreation yard in the prison had dozens of patches in the fence where inmates had tried to hacksaw their way to freedom.

Death row inmates routinely obtained hacksaw blades taken from prison workshops by inmates from the general population.

They traded drugs, cigarettes, and other contraband, as well as commissary items for the blades.

It turned out that death row inmates who were given work privileges had way too much freedom to move about unescorted by guards.

Gurule's escape alarmed the prosecutors who had sent him to death row. They worried he was headed back to exact revenge, and they beefed up their personal security.

A Sneaky Wily Man

The lead prosecutor described Gurule as "a sneaky, wily man" who had tried to break out of a holding cell during his murder trial back in 1993.

The Nueces County District Attorney told reporters he was unsurprised that Gurule was the first man to escape from death row since 1934. "I always thought that there was no way they could escape from death row. . . . But if I were to put money on it, I'd think Gurule would escape. He's very deceptive. If anyone could talk his way out of something, it's him."

Gurule's incarcerated girlfriend told reporters that he was deathly afraid of needles and did not want to die by lethal injection.

A Corpus Christi woman who dated Gurule for three years and testified for the prosecution during his trial stated, "He probably wants to go out in a blaze of glory. He's not one to sit and take it. I think he'd rather die being shot in the back running away than on a death chamber gurney."

Where's Gurule?

By nightfall of the third day of his escape, 500 searchers had failed to find a single clue.

They scoured the rugged 17,000-acre terrain around the prison.

The chase wore out seventy bloodhounds who couldn't pick up Garule's scent.

Officers stood watch every 25 yards along six miles of farm roads and state highways near the prison.

They checked every passing vehicle and opened every trunk lid.

Bold news headlines posed the question, "Where's Gurule?"

He became a hero for inmates who wanted a taste of freedom.

Prison officials flew in a Texas National Guard Helicopter equipped with heat-seeking cameras to help.

They hopefully speculated that Gurule must be hungry, sleep-deprived, bitten by insects or, worse yet, snakes, and was just one mistake away from getting caught.

False sightings came in of Gurule at a roadside park, drinking in a beer joint and in a church where the congregation prayed for him.

Wanted Dead or Alive

Alan Polunsky, the prison board chairman, vowed that Gurule would be captured "dead or alive."

Then Governor George W. Bush, with presidential aspirations and back from a trip to the Middle East, angrily demanded to know how Gurule had escaped and called in the Texas Rangers to investigate.

The Governor's office posted wanted posters across the state offering a $5,000 reward.

The escape became a political hot potato.

A week into the manhunt, Texas announced that they were preparing to execute Gurule's fellow death row escapees.

And then, two prison workers fishing on their day off discovered a bloated body floating in a river about a mile away from the prison.

Drowned in Freedom's Waters

Condemned killer Martin Gurule did not get very far. His body was still wrapped in a makeshift cardboard vest with magazines strapped to his arms and legs with elastic bandages.

Weighted by his water-logged shield from razor wire, Gurule plunged to the bottom after stumbling into the swamp beside the prison.

Gurule had a superficial wound from a guard's bullet that creased his back.

An autopsy concluded that Gurule drowned shortly after his escape.

A Legacy of Change

Later, an investigation blamed the death row escape on negligent guards and poor security.

Guards failed to use flashlights to check sleeping death row inmates and mistook the makeshift dummies for humans.

Too many guards took the night off or left early for Thanksgiving, leaving recreation yards and cellblocks improperly supervised.

Neither a special motion-detector fence nor security cameras worked, the latter because somebody forgot to put a tape into the VCR.

And when one tower guard spotted the convicts running toward the perimeter fence, he stopped to extinguish his cigarette before opening fire.

Demotions and terminations followed.

In the wake of Gurule's escape, a year later, death row was moved to the wing of a newly built maximum security prison.

The prison system abolished the death row work program.

It changed the name of the new death row prison to the Polunsky Unit.

Named after the prison official who vowed that Martin Gurule would be caught dead or alive.

The Killer on The Family Tree

When you search for your family roots, you never know what you might find on your family tree.

Veteran Texas lawman Louis Fawcett found an uncle at the center of a sensational murder trial in 1935.

It was so notorious that schoolchildren were paraded through the Liberty County jail on macabre field trips to get a look at the accused killers.

It was called the Ride Murder.

Fawcett had spent 43 years hunting down criminals for the Texas Prison System and the FBI.

The Shocking Discovery

Suddenly, his genealogical hobby discovered that his uncle was the triggerman in the Ride Murder.

Fawcett is disappointed that the victim's family did not receive justice. "They never had any peace. Because of that death. And this is one of the things that troubles me about this particular case."

Louis Fawcett was a renowned fugitive hunter for the Texas Prison System and served on task forces for the FBI and U.S. Marshals Service.

A Sensational Crime and a Public Spectacle

As a kid, he heard stories that his uncle was a killer. So, he started digging into his family tree at the local library. Another genealogical researcher overheard Fawcett's request and revealed that she saw his uncle when her elementary school class visited the jail on a field trip when she was eleven years old.

Fawcett's search led him to a murder committed on February 12, 1935.

The bullet-riddled, partially clad body of an unidentified man was found in a muddy ditch thirty-one miles from the Port of Houston.

That set Fawcett on a quest to identify the shooting victim.

"I want to get him returned to his family or at least get some resolution so we can get a headstone for his grave. It's important to me and to the victims of crime to be able to have some resolution."

An Unidentified Victim

The murder victim was a seaman without a name or birthplace.

Stocky build. Between 28 and 30 years of age. 155 pounds. Five feet nine inches tall.

He had a scar three-fourths of an inch long behind his right ear and a growth the size of a quarter located an inch above his forehead.

The victim was found in his underwear, wearing a shirt, one glove, and a tie tightly drawn under his shirt into his mouth.

His body smelled of liquor. In a macabre display, residents and school kids lined up to see his body laid out in the morgue.

The death certificate ruled the cause of death as shot with a .32 caliber pistol 5 times.

- Twice in the right side lower ribs.
- Once in the right side shoulder blade.
- Once in the right side of the neck.

And once in the right temple by an unknown party or parties.

According to the newspaper reports, his name was Mancuso. Fawcett thought that was the victim's first name but later learned it was his last name. The seaman was from Buenos Aires, and the ship he sailed on was flagged in Italy. And that's all it was ever learned about him.

The murder remained a mystery, a cold case for two years.

A Confession and an Accusation

In 1937, a confession by Richard Palmer summoned the Liberty County Sheriff to Austin, Texas.

The 26-year-old Palmer was being held on a life sentence for a similar "ride murder" of a Houston salesman.

Palmer confessed to the murder of the unidentified man and named John Wesley "Blackie" Fawcett as his accomplice.

Then 25-year-old Blackie Fawcett was the uncle of the lawman Louis Fawcett.

Palmer said the victim was a seaman named Mancuso. They met him at a Houston dice game. He appeared to have some money. Fawcett picks up the story, "They put him in a car. They recruited a woman in her early twenties to lure Mancuso into their car. They bought a lot of alcohol. And drove around drinking and partying and talking."

The Woman in The Quilt

Palmer told the Sheriff they plied the seaman with whiskey. A witness told police that a mystery woman with red hair was in the back seat wrapped in a quilt beside a man who was "beastly drunk or dead."

Officers found the mystery woman, 22-year-old Mrs. Nellie Scoville, in Oklahoma and arrested her for murder.

They also arrested Palmer and Blackie Fawcett for murder.

Fawcett says the accused killers became the subject of morbid school field trips to the county jail. "They actually saw my uncle, and they saw Palmer, who had drawn sketches of both signed by each.

Panic In the Courtroom

Palmer's murder trial got off to a rocky start when someone cried out that Palmer was trying to escape.

Texas Rangers pulled their guns. Deputies rushed to the exits. Officers crashed into the Sheriff's office only to find Palmer seated calmly in a chair facing his attorney.

Nellie Scoville, the mystery woman, was the star witness in Palmer's murder trial.

A Clever Defense Strategy

A hush fell over the packed courtroom as she gave a gruesome description of how she accompanied Palmer and

Fawcett on the "death ride" and saw them throw the body out of the car.

She claimed Fawcett was the trigger man. But in a moment of courtroom theater, Fawcett's defense attorney Price Daniel, an up-and-coming politician, summoned a slender, dark-haired man before the witness stand.

Price Daniel asked Scoville to identify the man. She testified that he was "Blackie" Fawcett. But he was a ringer. "My uncle had jet-black hair. Thus they called him "Blackie. "So they brought in a guy who was a wholesale grocer and resembled Fawcett. The accused female accomplice mistakenly picked him out as one of the killers. And, of course, that got my uncle off," said Fawcett.

Palmer was found guilty and received a life sentence for murder.

Prosecutors were determined to send Fawcett to the Texas electric chair, known as "Old Sparky."

Fawcett had confessed to riding around with Palmer and the seaman. He claimed they got drunk and decided to rob him. Fawcett claimed Palmer was the triggerman and divided $140 taken from the seaman's pocket after the shooting.

But Fawcett later recanted the confession and claimed he signed it out of fear of bodily harm from officers.

A Mistrial and Repeated Trials

The judge declared a mistrial when the Sheriff disclosed in his testimony that Fawcett had served four months in the Louisiana prison system for auto theft.

When Fawcett was retried, the jury deadlocked after 70 hours because one of the 12 jury members held out for a 25-year sentence. The other eleven voted to send Fawcett to the electric chair.

The judge declared a mistrial and sent the jury home.

In a third and final murder trial, the jury found Fawcett not guilty.

Fawcett took the stand in his defense.

Fawcett's mother and other family members testified that he was home at the time of the murder. And a police chief confirmed that Fawcett had stopped by to see him.

Nellie Scoville's misidentification in the earlier murder trial clearly influenced the jury's decision to acquit Fawcett.

They deliberated for less than two hours.

Wesley "Blackie" Fawcett walked out of the Liberty County courthouse a free man on November 9, 1938.

An Accomplice's Mysterious Death

A year after the trial, his alleged accomplice, Richard A. Palmer, twice convicted of murder, was killed in a predawn mystery stabbing at the Retrieve Prison Farm outside Houston.

The lifer was stabbed a half dozen times as inmates lined up to work in the fields.

He staggered into the prison hospital, where he died without saying a word.

The knife was never found. The inmates sealed their lips in a code of prison silence.

Was the prison hit payback for snitching on Blackie Fawcett?

A Lawman's Lingering Doubt

Though decades have passed since the "Ride Murder," its shadow still lingers over Liberty County and, in a more personal way, over Louis Fawcett. The veteran lawman may have spent a lifetime pursuing justice, but he remains haunted by a crime rooted within his family tree. His uncle, Wesley "Blackie" Fawcett, escaped the electric chair, but not the violence that marked his final days. And while Blackie's life ended in a fiery accident, the true identity of his victim—a seaman without a name or a family to mourn him—remains lost to time.

Seeking Relatives for an Unnamed Victim

Now, Louis Fawcett, the one-time fugitive hunter, has turned his pursuit inward, seeking answers for the unnamed man found lifeless in a muddy ditch all those years ago. Despite the grim discoveries about his uncle, Fawcett holds to the hope that, through modern DNA testing, the seaman's family might one day be found and that a proper resting place can be given to the man lost in a web of betrayal and greed.

In the end, Fawcett's journey serves as a reminder that family secrets often bring only heartbreak—and that sometimes, no matter how hard we seek closure, some stories are destined to end without answers.

Vanished into Mystery's Shadow: The Story of Charles J. Woods

The tale of Charles J. Woods—a bank robber, prison escapee, and a man who lived under a web of aliases—is a Texas legend wrapped in layers of mystery, escape, and conspiracy. Woods' life spiraled into a realm of intrigue typically reserved for spy novels, one filled with encounters that suggest deeper ties to covert operations in the twilight shadows of Cold War America. From his audacious prison escape to his reported connections to the infamous Mena, Arkansas airport, Woods' story leaves us with more questions than answers.

Louis Fawcett, a resolute fugitive hunter for the Texas prison system, was among the few determined enough to follow Woods' trail, years after his escape. His relentless pursuit would eventually lead him to an airport in Mena, Arkansas— an airport rumored to be a hub for illicit activities involving drug smuggling and CIA dealings. For Fawcett, this was no ordinary pursuit; he was stepping into a murky world of interwoven crime and conspiracy.

"Mena, Arkansas, was a place where the CIA, I believe, had an undercover operation of some sort," Fawcett shared during a reflective interview years later. "It sent up a red flag because here's a guy working in Oklahoma with a government-style ID card with an alias name on it—and he's going to Mena, Arkansas." His voice, a mix of suspicion and intrigue, underscored the shadows that hovered over Woods' story.

Fawcett's suspicions fueled his investigation, but the deeper he dug, the more elusive Woods became.

The Beginnings of Charles J. Woods: A Complex Childhood

Charles J. Woods was born in 1933 in Rock Island, Illinois. His childhood was troubled and fractured. When his parents separated, his father resorted to kidnapping Woods and his younger brother, hiding them with an elderly couple deep in a swamp. This dark start to his life paints a picture of early instability that likely shaped his later defiance of societal norms. Eventually, the police intervened, reuniting the boys with their mother. She moved them to Dallas, Texas, in 1943, where Woods would spend his formative years.

Woods would later describe himself as a generally cheerful individual, striving to make the best of any situation. Yet, his resentment toward his mother simmered beneath the surface. He felt stifled, "tied to her apron strings," as he would later tell a prison psychologist. His frustrations eventually ignited, leading him down a dark path that would come to define his life.

As a young man, Woods developed a work ethic that could have paved the way to a successful career. He worked tirelessly, taking on odd jobs, including a 10-year stint as a paperboy. Rising at 4:30 each morning, Woods threw newspapers into the yards of homes along his route, developing the grit and determination he would later use in his criminal life. His early hobbies included hunting, fishing, and gun collecting—interests that foreshadowed the darker turns his life would eventually take. By high school, he had earned a private pilot's license with the Civil Air Patrol, foreshadowing his later criminal exploits involving flights across state lines.

It was an ill-fated 1940 Ford Coupe, an oil-burning car he bought for $400, that pushed Woods toward crime. When the car broke down, he found himself in need of $1,000 to replace the motor. His stepfather, who had helped him pick out the car, refused to lend him the money, setting the stage for Woods' first foray into criminality. Desperation drove him to pick up a gun.

The Calculated Descent into Crime

Woods' descent began with a cold determination. He pulled his first armed robbery at a small grocery store in the Oak Cliff section of Dallas. It was around 9 p.m. when the teenage Woods walked in, armed with a .32 caliber automatic pistol, and demanded cash. He left with $100, his mind already calculating his next steps. To him, crime was a mathematical problem; he needed money, and robbery seemed the quickest solution.

Later, Woods set his sights on 7-11 stores, learning they kept more cash on hand and were typically unguarded. He managed to steal approximately $600 through a series of stickups, but he remained short of the $1,000 he needed for his car. By now, he was becoming well-practiced, described by store clerks as "determined" and "cool." But a witness took down his license plate number, and Woods was soon arrested.

"I guess I did it because I had a good reputation," Woods later admitted. "I knew no one would suspect me, and I had it figured out mathematically." To Woods, his logic seemed irrefutable. But his parents and neighbors were shocked. They couldn't reconcile the image of the easy-going, good-natured young man with that of a criminal. Even the son of the Dallas Police Chief, a close friend of Woods, couldn't believe the charges against him. Through some connections, Woods' charge was reduced, and he was sentenced to a five-year prison term in 1951.

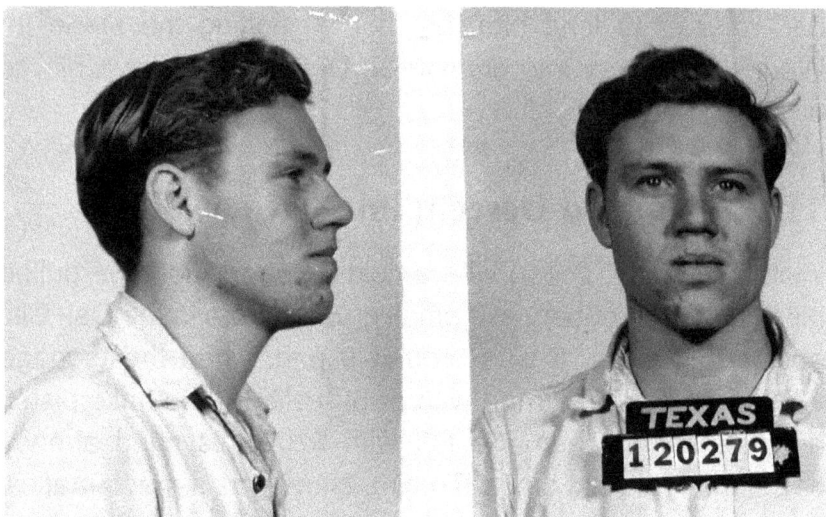

Charles J. Woods 1951 Mug Shot

Once inside, Woods underwent psychological evaluations. Prison psychologists found him emotionally paralyzed and noted schizophrenic trends, but they also noted his strong mechanical aptitude. Woods seemed a paradox—a man who could repair machines but struggled to connect with other people.

A Chance at Redemption

After serving a year, Woods received a full pardon, owing largely to the support of figures in the local school district and community members who saw potential in him. He returned to the outside world with hopes of making a fresh start, enrolling at the University of Oklahoma, where he earned a degree in geology. He even joined the Air Force Reserve and took a job in Anchorage, Alaska, as a geologist. Yet, despite his academic and career achievements, the thrill of crime continued to beckon.

His niece, Vicki Holder, recalled that her uncle harbored dreams of farming. "Chuck wanted to be a farmer in Honduras," she remembered. "He convinced my father to join him. They set up a farm, bought equipment, and prepared to harvest cotton. But the political climate changed, and rebels forced them to flee." By the time they returned to Texas, Woods' financial resources had dwindled. In a state of desperation, he found himself resorting once again to crime.

Back to Crime: A Bank Robbery and a Second Sentence

This time, Woods' target was Airline State Bank in Houston. Arriving by plane from Dallas, he rented a car, drove to the bank, and approached the teller with a pistol. He left with $7,500 in cash, but a high-speed chase ensued, and he was arrested. Vicki Holder later described her uncle as something of an "adrenaline junkie." His impulsive decisions and desire for adventure became part of his identity, and they would eventually lead him back into the Texas prison system, this time with a 25-year sentence.

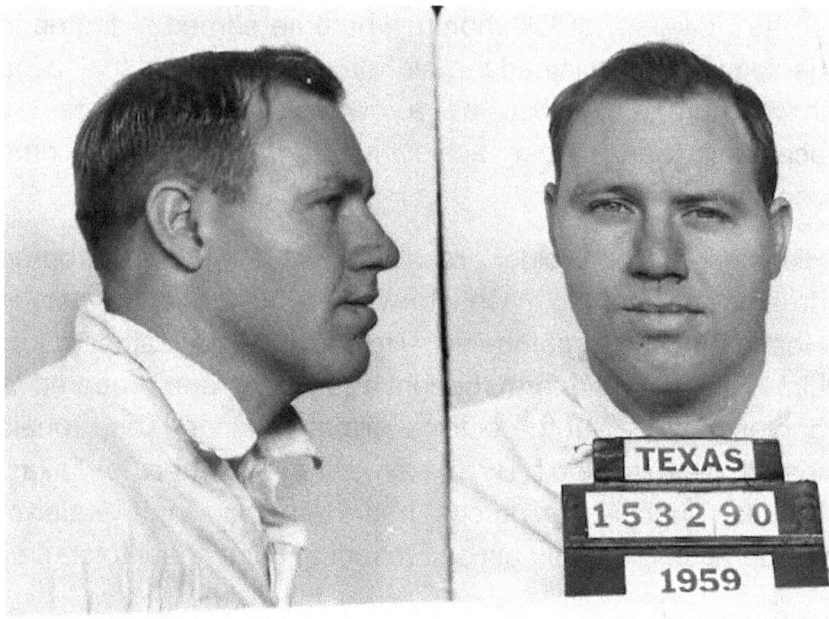

Charles J. Woods 1959 Mug Shot

Eastham Unit, the maximum-security prison where Woods was sent, was notorious among inmates and guards alike. Known as "The Ham," the facility had once held Clyde Barrow of the infamous Bonnie and Clyde duo. A new psychological evaluation painted Woods as selfish and self-centered, with ambitions that exceeded his abilities. Yet, he again managed to maneuver his way into a trusted position, this time as a surveyor on a construction crew.

Louis Fawcett later noted, "He convinced the warden he was a surveyor and got assigned to work outside the prison. He was charming and persuasive, and he had a knack for getting people to trust him."

The Great Escape

In May of 1961, Woods made his move. He convinced prison officials to assign him to a construction survey crew outside the prison walls, positioning himself for an escape. On October 26, 1961, while working on a road near the Ellis I Maximum Security Unit, he and another inmate took a guard hostage. After tying him up, they fled in a prison truck.

Woods was eventually spotted near Point Blank, Texas, but managed to evade capture. Family lore tells of Woods using a reed to breathe while hiding underwater, eluding search dogs and guards alike. According to his niece, "He hid in the woods and breathed through a reed while search parties and dogs scoured the area. He waited it out until they abandoned the hunt."

A Life on the Run

Once he felt the coast was clear, Woods made his way back to Dallas, where he reached out to his brother for assistance. Together, they disposed of the stolen vehicle and set Woods up in a new life in Little Rock, Arkansas. From there, he adopted the alias Richard Arthur Mills, eventually relocating to Tulsa, Oklahoma, where he married under his new identity. He continued to evade detection, blending into society under his new persona.

Fawcett's investigations into Woods' past revealed that he had even acquired a government-issued ID in Oklahoma, which allowed him to work at the Naval Ammunition Depot in McAlester, Oklahoma. It was here that his connections to Mena, Arkansas, and the broader web of conspiracy would deepen.

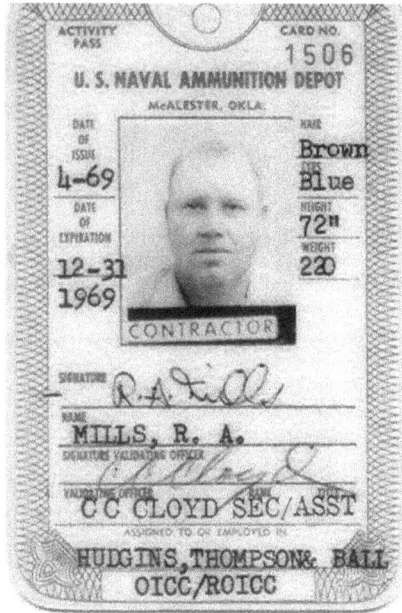

Richard Arthur Mills aka Charles Woods
Naval Ammunition Depot ID Card

Mena, Arkansas: The Heart of the Conspiracy

During the 1980s, Mena, Arkansas, became infamous as a hotbed of rumor and conspiracy. With its remote location and proximity to the Ouachita Mountains, it was the perfect cover for clandestine operations. In this secluded spot, Barry Seal— a former airline pilot turned drug smuggler—established a base for his vast narcotics enterprise, allegedly shuttling drugs for the Medellín Cartel and later working with the DEA. Seal's connection to Mena fostered theories that the CIA was using the small town's airstrip for covert operations involving drug running to fund anti-Sandinista rebels in Nicaragua.

For a fugitive like Charles J. Woods, Mena's under-the-radar status and possible ties to covert operations provided a unique hiding place and, potentially, a means to fund his life on the run. Louis Fawcett was one of the first to draw a link between Woods and Mena, believing that Woods may have taken advantage of the airport's covert nature to continue his criminal activities.

"He was going to Mena, Arkansas, in that area," Fawcett explained. "He was likely robbing banks to make a living. His brother told me they had a pickup truck kept in a hangar at the airport, and they'd use it to travel around when they flew into Mena. The whole setup struck me as strange."

The Double Life of "Richard Mills"

Under his new alias, Richard Arthur Mills, Woods led a remarkably ordinary life for a time. He worked as an engineering inspector, living in the Oklahoma City suburb of Midwest City. He became a Boy Scout leader, attended St. Matthew's Methodist Church, and earned the trust of his neighbors and colleagues. His idyllic suburban life starkly contrasted with the life of crime he had once led, yet for Woods, this was merely a temporary reprieve.

"He was a good friend to one of the local government officials," Fawcett noted, describing the connections Woods, as Mills, made in the local community. "They would go flying together. The company he worked for had a plane, and he and others would fly to Mena on fishing trips. But from everything I'd learned, I suspect those trips involved more than just fishing."

The ties between Woods, Mena, and the suspicions of illegal activity grew murkier. Fawcett speculated that Woods may have used the Mena airport as a launchpad for bank robberies across the country, using his alias and connections to cover his tracks. In mid-November 1969, however, Woods' life took a fatal turn.

The Final Flight: A Crash in the Mountains

Woods, still known to his neighbors as Richard Mills, was flying a single-engine Cessna 172 from Mount Ida, Arkansas, to McAlester, Oklahoma, on a stormy day in 1969. Not instrument-rated and likely unfamiliar with the challenging weather conditions, he struggled to control the plane in a violent thunderstorm. As he attempted to climb over Black Fork Mountain, he clipped the tops of pine trees and then collided with a massive cedar, tearing the wings from the fuselage and throwing the engine—and Woods himself—from the plane.

Fawcett uncovered these details during his investigation, which included examining the crash site. "Mena was known to be a place for CIA covert operations," he explained. "But that was years later. Still, it raised suspicions because this guy had a government-style ID card with an alias name, and his fingerprint was on the back. I verified it was his fingerprint, so I knew he had been operating under an assumed identity."

Despite Fawcett's suspicions, the crash marked the end of Woods' fugitive years. Officially, he was dead, though his legacy of crime and conspiracy was far from forgotten.

The Unraveling of Mena's Secrets

Years after Woods' death, Mena, Arkansas, would again capture public attention. In 1998, journalist Sarah McClendon questioned President Bill Clinton during a press conference, pointing to the alleged CIA-backed drug-running operation in

Mena during Clinton's governorship of Arkansas. The query reignited a flurry of speculation around the town's murky past and the alleged collusion of government agencies with narcotics traffickers to fund covert operations.

"The Republicans are trying to blame you for the existence of a small air base at Mena, Arkansas," McClendon charged, hinting at government involvement. Clinton dismissed the allegations, claiming it was "primarily a matter for federal jurisdiction." Yet, her question furthered the theory that the Mena airport had been a focal point for covert dealings during the height of the Iran-Contra affair.

These suspicions were fueled by the life and death of Barry Seal, who, like Woods, had used Mena as a base for his nefarious operations. Seal, a former CIA operative with ties to the Medellín Cartel, was believed to have shuttled millions of dollars worth of cocaine into the U.S. He became a government informant after his 1983 arrest, providing information on the cartel leaders and participating in elaborate sting operations, including one with CIA-installed cameras on his plane that captured Sandinista officials loading drugs. Seal's role as both a criminal and an informant only added to the complexity of Mena's shadowy reputation.

A Life of Secrets Revealed

The story of Charles J. Woods remained unknown to many, but to those who knew him as Richard Mills, the revelation of his true identity after the fatal plane crash was devastating. His wife, who had known nothing of his criminal past, was left to grapple with the truth. Vicki Holder, Woods' niece, described the impact of the revelation on his widow, who learned only after his death that her husband's real name was not Richard Mills.

"She was very upset," Holder remembered. "My aunt and my father sat her down after the funeral and explained his background. She was in mourning, pregnant with their second child. It was a terrible shock."

Legacy of Shadows: A Reporter's Final Thoughts

In the aftermath of his death, Charles J. Woods' life raised questions that remain unanswered. Could he have been involved in the covert operations surrounding Mena? Was his life merely that of a bank robber and escape artist, or did he have a deeper role in the conspiracies that shrouded Mena, Arkansas? As with many legends, the story of Woods leaves us with fragments of truth interwoven with the shadows of conspiracy.

Reflecting on my reporting experiences during the 1980s, I recall my time covering the Texas National Guard's exercises near the Nicaraguan border, a symbol of President Ronald Reagan's aggression against the Sandinista regime. It was during this era that Seal's C-123K cargo plane—once used in CIA operations—was shot down over Nicaragua, exposing the U.S. government's covert involvement in the Iran-Contra affair. For a brief moment, the veil lifted, revealing glimpses of hidden operations conducted in secret.

Years later, in 1996, the CIA admitted that it had conducted a joint training operation at the Mena airport with another federal agency, though it denied involvement in drug trafficking or other illegal activities. The CIA's Inspector General found "no evidence" linking the agency to arms smuggling, drug running, or other alleged crimes at Mena. Yet, to conspiracy theorists and those familiar with Mena's legacy, the shadows remain.

Ultimately, the story of Charles J. Woods, alias Richard Arthur Mills, exemplifies the allure and danger of leading a double life. In Woods, we find the enduring paradox of a man who once charmed his way to freedom, only to find himself forever ensnared in a cycle of deception and pursuit. For fugitive hunter Louis Fawcett, the trail may have ended with Woods' death, but the questions linger, inviting each of us to peer into the mystery's shadow.

Beneath The Charm: Unveiling Texas Black Widow

Amidst the sprawling cityscape of Dallas, where power and prosperity intersect with secrets and lies, Sandra Bridewell's story unravels.

Bridewell was a beautiful, alluring socialite in the affluent enclave of Highland Park when Dallas was the world's most popular TV show and the Dallas Cowboys were America's team.

It is a tale woven with deception, sex, and the dark underbelly of high society in a close-knit community known as the Beverly Hills of the Southwest -- Highland Park.

Known infamously as "The Black Widow," Sandra's life story reads like a script from a classic thriller, her charm, and beauty masking a sinister reality of purported suicides, murders, beatings, romance scams, religious cons, and identity theft.

A "Black Widow" Unmasked

True Crime author John Leake peeled back the layers of Sandra Bridewell's enigmatic persona in The Meaning of Malice: On The Trail Of The Black Widow Of Highland Park.

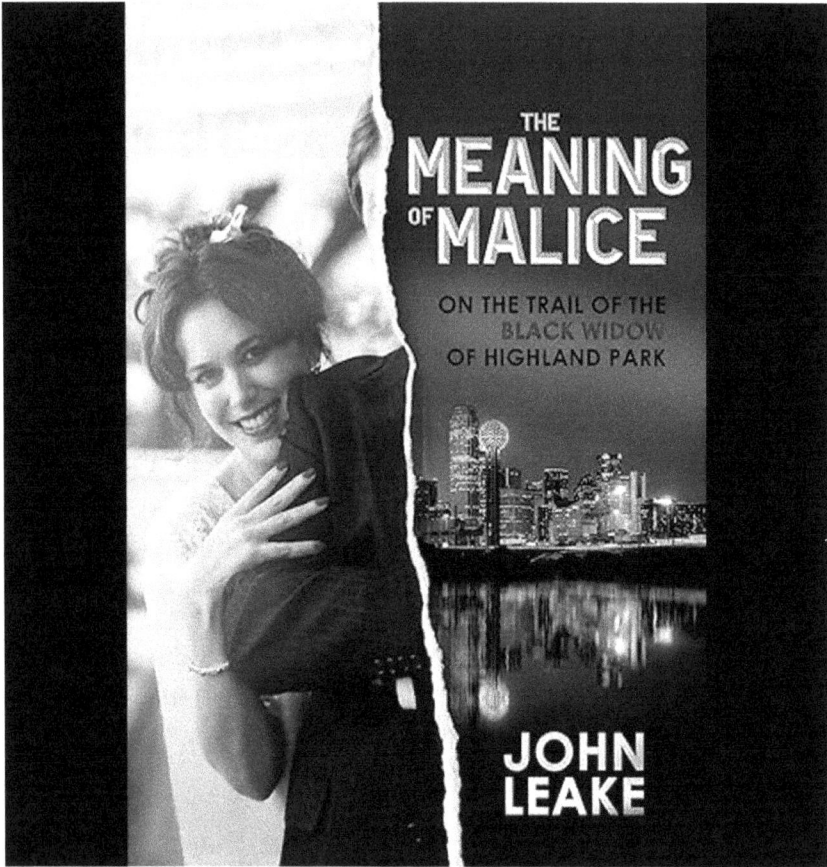

Sandra Bridewell "The Black Widow"

The story of Sandra Bridewell has captivated and horrified Dallas society for decades. As I delved deeper into the case, speaking with those who knew her and examining the evidence, a chilling picture began to emerge of a woman who may have been far more dangerous than anyone initially realized.

John Leake spent years investigating Sandra Bridewell's life, and shared his disturbing conclusions with me. "After evaluating all of the evidence, both circumstantial and physical, I believe Sandra Bridewell is not only a Black Widow but an officially undetected serial killer," Leake told me gravely.

He explained that the first two violent deaths connected to Bridewell - in 1975 and 1982 were initially ruled suicides by the Dallas County Medical Examiner. However, when Leake obtained copies of the death scene photos years later and had them examined by contemporary forensic experts, a very different story emerged.

"The evidence displayed in the photos shows that these were not self-inflicted deaths," Leake said. "There was another party involved." He went on to describe how the physical evidence in the photos, combined with circumstantial evidence and witness testimony, led him to his chilling conclusion about Bridewell.

What makes the case so shocking is that despite long being suspected of involvement in multiple deaths, Sandra Bridewell has never been arrested or even subjected to a difficult interview by law enforcement. She has managed to elude justice for decades, leaving a trail of destruction in her wake.

Early Life and Ambition

To understand how Sandra Bridewell became the infamous "Black Widow" of Highland Park Texas, we have to go back to her beginnings. She arrived in Dallas as a child in 1950, after her mother had been killed in a car accident. It was a tragic start to a life that would be marked by death and misfortune - much of it, investigators now believe, orchestrated by Sandra herself.

Sandra's early life was far from the glittering world of Dallas high society she would later inhabit. Her father's soft drink bottling business had fallen on hard times, and he lost his leg in a hunting accident. He remarried and began selling cemetery plots to make ends meet.

Young Sandra did not get along with her new stepmother. More significantly, she developed a burning desire to escape her working-class neighborhood of South Oak Cliff, located across the Trinity River from downtown Dallas. This yearning to elevate her social status would become a defining force in Sandra's life, driving her to pursue wealthy men and the trappings of high society at any cost.

Despite her humble beginnings, Sandra received a solid education at Kimball High School in Oak Cliff. Interestingly, this was the same school attended by blues legend Stevie Ray Vaughan just a year after Sandra. While Oak Cliff was not necessarily a rough neighborhood, it was certainly perceived as humble compared to the exclusive enclaves Sandra aspired to inhabit.

John Leake, in our conversations, emphasized how crucial understanding Sandra's background is to grasp her later actions. "Given what we now know about Sandra's social aspirations," he told me, "I think Oak Cliff was perceived by her as a humble neighborhood she desperately wanted to escape."

This desire to elevate her social status seems to have ignited in Sandra's imagination at a young age. Dallas in the 1950s and 60s was a city defined by stark contrasts between old money and new oil wealth, with institutions like Neiman Marcus and the Dallas Cowboys representing the pinnacle of glamour and success.

The Cinderella Syndrome

"There was an article in *D Magazine* about the 'Cinderella syndrome' that seems so prevalent in Dallas culture," Leake explained. "Something about the culture here - Neiman Marcus, the Dallas Cowboys, the Murchisons, the Hunts - seems to promote this Cinderella aspiration of a pretty girl marrying a rich man. This idea really ignited in Sandra's imagination."

Sandra saw herself as beautiful and talented, with knowledge of French cooking, culture, and interior decorating. She became fixated on the idea of finding a wealthy man to elevate her status and provide the lifestyle she craved.

Her first attempt at social climbing came when she attended Tyler Junior College in the early 1960s. Located in the heart of the East Texas oil patch, where huge fortunes had been made, Tyler seemed like the perfect hunting ground for a young woman seeking to land a wealthy oil heir. Though she didn't succeed in Tyler, this experience likely shaped her later pursuits.

"The interesting thing," Leake noted, "is that while she didn't find her oil heir in Tyler, she eventually married into an oil family years later when she wed Bobby Bridewell, who came from a Tyler, Texas oil family."

Oil Wealth

The oil money from the East Texas fields had a profound impact on Dallas, flowing into exclusive neighborhoods like Highland Park. Surrounded by the city of Dallas but existing as a separate municipality, Highland Park became known as the "Beverly Hills of the Southwest." Today, it remains home to some of the wealthiest and most influential people in Texas, including Jerry Jones, owner of the Dallas Cowboys.

What many people don't realize, Leake told me, is that Highland Park shares more than just a reputation with Beverly Hills - it was actually designed by the same landscape architect. "David Wilbur Cook, who was the landscape designer for Beverly Hills, also did the layout for Highland Park," Leake explained. "So it's a very apt comparison."

This was the rarefied world Sandra Bridewell was determined to infiltrate. Her path to Highland Park society began in the 1960s in an apartment complex called the Spanish Trace, located near Southern Methodist University.

The Spanish Trace was more than just an apartment building - it was a scene, a place where the young, beautiful, and affluent gathered to see and be seen. The developers had connections with Eddie Ackerman, the CEO of Braniff Airlines, and through this relationship, they arranged to have a certain number of apartments allocated to beautiful Braniff stewardesses.

"This was the 60s," Leake explained, painting a vivid picture of the era. "The Spanish Trace had a swimming pool and these gorgeous stewardesses living there, which in turn drew in the well-heeled, handsome young men."

The Social Climber's First Marriage

It was in this atmosphere of youthful glamour and ambition that Sandra met her first husband, David Stegall. Sandra was living in an apartment across the street from the Spanish Trace in a building called the Windsor House. David, a recent graduate of the Baylor School of Dentistry, lived at the Spanish Trace.

David Stegall wasn't just any dentist - he was studying with a famous reconstructive dentist in Beverly Hills, learning the art of creating perfect smiles for the camera. As Leake discovered in his research, David had even worked on Paul Newman's teeth during one of his trips to California.

"I'm partly speculating," Leake told me, "but I imagine he told Sandra about his aspirations to become a dentist to the stars. She likely found it very compelling."

The world Sandra was entering was one of high fashion and jet-set glamour, epitomized by Braniff Airlines. Braniff was revolutionizing air travel, turning it into a stylish experience with aircraft painted in eye-catching designs and flight attendants outfitted in fashions by famous designers.

"Salvador Dali was even a designer for Braniff," Leake noted, underscoring just how avant-garde and luxurious the airline aimed to be.

The standards for beauty and style were exacting. Flight attendants had to meet strict criteria, and even the slightest flaw could disqualify a candidate. "If a tooth didn't look just white enough, they didn't make the grade," I remarked to Leake.

He agreed, adding, "This was the early era of jet travel. Now we take it for granted, and it's often a bit of a beatdown. But in those days, it was new, it was glamorous."

Leake went on to describe how airlines like Braniff and Pan Am had partnerships with luxury hotel chains like Hilton, which was aggressively building properties in exotic locations like Acapulco, Mexico. The Spanish Trace apartments capitalized on this jet-set culture: "If you signed a one-year lease at the Trace, you were invited for the annual Acapulco bash, flown down on Braniff," Leake explained. "They were really cultivating this air of glamour and sex appeal."

For Sandra Bridewell, barely into her twenties, it must have seemed like she had hit the jackpot. She was living in the midst of this glamorous scene, surrounded by beautiful people and up-and-coming professionals. And now she had caught the eye of David Stegall, a promising young dentist with dreams of Hollywood success.

However, as Leake's investigation revealed, Sandra's expectations were wildly unrealistic. She seemed to have no concept of the financial realities of a dentist's income compared to someone working in oil, gas, real estate, or banking.

"One of the first things Sandra did after marrying David was purchase a house in Greenway Parks, which is immediately adjacent to Highland Park," Leake told me. "It's also a very beautiful neighborhood."

But Sandra wasn't content with just any nice house. She hired John Astin Perkins, a Yale-trained art historian and interior designer, to decorate their new home. Perkins was no ordinary decorator - he was the designer for some of Dallas's most prominent figures, including Ross Perot and Clint Murchison, the owner of the Dallas Cowboys.

"Quite quickly, David realizes, 'Wow, this interior design project - antiques, tapestries, original oil paintings - is outstripping my income,'" Leake explained.

Sandra's extravagant spending habits would become a recurring theme in her relationships. Leake titled one chapter in his book "A Black Belt in Home Decorating," borrowing a phrase used by oil tycoon Clint Murchison Sr. to describe his first wife's shopping habits.

"Clint's first wife would go to Neiman Marcus and literally buy every single dress in her size," Leake recounted. "She'd just clean out the joint. And, of course, Clint Murchison possessed an enormous oil fortune, so he could afford it."

Sandra, it seemed, had similar tastes but without the multimillion-dollar bank account to back them up. "Sandra had a black belt in shopping as well," Leake noted, "But home decorating was really her thing. And she had a black belt in it for sure."

This era of Sandra's life coincided with a boom time for Dallas. The 1973 Arab-Israeli War led to an oil embargo, causing oil prices to skyrocket. Between 1974 and 1980, the price per barrel shot up to over $100.

"These independent oil and gas companies in Dallas, provided they had good leases at the time, were suddenly coining money," Leake explained. "It's interesting because this was an era of stagflation in the United States as a whole, so Dallas really was standing out as a bright spot in the American economy."

The city's prosperity, combined with the glamour of the Dallas Cowboys (known as "America's Team") and luxury retailers like Neiman Marcus, caught the attention of Hollywood. In 1978, the same year Sandra married her second husband, Bobby Bridewell, the first episode of the hit TV series "Dallas" was filmed.

A Suspicious "Suicide"

But before Sandra could move on to her second marriage, there was the matter of her first husband, David Stegall. By the beginning of 1975, Sandra had driven the young dentist to the brink of bankruptcy. He was deeply in debt and serious financial trouble.

Then, suddenly, Sandra phoned a friend with shocking news: something terrible had happened to David.

What happened next would set the pattern for much of Sandra's life - a mysterious death followed by behavior that raised eyebrows among those who knew her. Leake's investigation uncovered disturbing details about the events surrounding David Stegall's death.

"Before she called the police," Leake told me, his voice grave, "Sandra called some friends. A prominent dentist who knew David, I believe she called maybe another medical man as well."

These friends rushed over to the Stegall home, entering the bedroom where David lay dead before the police had even been notified. When I asked Leake about the purpose of these calls, he could only speculate, but he believed Sandra was "putting a layer of insulation between her and the police."

"When the police arrived, she's sort of beside herself with emotion," Leake explained. "And these men are there to assist in establishing her social bona fide. These are serious guys, medical professionals, prominent people in the community."

The result, according to Leake, was that law enforcement perceived Sandra as a "socially integrated woman" from the start. This perception seemed to preclude any serious inquiry or examination of the circumstances surrounding David's death.

"They survey the death scene in the marital bed," Leake continued. "Apparently, at the time, it sort of looked like suicide, like he'd shot himself in bed. The medical examiner did not perform an autopsy, and he only performed an external examination."

Years later, when Leake obtained the external examination report and the death scene photos, he found that they told a very different story than that of a straightforward suicide.

"The first thing I noticed just reading the external exam report," Leake said, "was on his forearm, nowhere near where the radial artery comes up into the wrist where you take the pulse, but like the forearm proper, where the muscle and a lot of fascia tissue is, the medical examiner describes these relatively superficial incisions."

These cuts on David's arm were presented as evidence that he had tried to commit suicide by cutting himself before resorting to the gun. But to Leake, this scenario made little sense.

"Why would he slash himself on the forearm?" Leake questioned. "I spoke to some of his old dental buddies who were still alive. David had studied anatomy for a year at the Baylor School of Dentistry. He knew this would have no lethal effect. It would be painful, it would be upsetting and distressing to cut oneself on the forearm, but he knew that it would have no lethal effect."

The death scene photos revealed even more inconsistencies. "You can see from the blood stain pattern he never moved," Leake explained. "His right arm never moved, so it's not like he climbs into bed with a razor, slashes himself, thinks to himself, 'Oh no, I'm not bleeding out. I'm gonna have to go find the pistol.' The bloodstain shows he got into bed with a loaded and cocked pistol, was lying there, and never moved."

Leake laid out the implausibility of the suicide scenario: "If you follow the logic of this, I'm gonna get into bed with a pistol ready to go, the cartridge chambered. But before I shoot myself in the head, I'm going to slash myself to no lethal effect on the right forearm? I just found that strange."

But the most damning evidence, in Leake's view, came from the position of the body and the bedding. "The first thing you notice is he's been tucked in," Leake said. "The way the bedding is tucked along the backside of his legs, the backside of his buttocks, someone has smoothed out the comforter on the right side of the bed and then tucked him in. The comforter is drawn up over his left hand, lying outstretched on the weapon."

Leake emphasized the impossibility of this scenario if it were truly a suicide: "It's impossible to shoot yourself in the left side of the head with the pistol, have the hand then fall on the bed, and then draw the covers up. That's impossible."

The origin of the gun used in David's death added another layer of suspicion. Leake's investigation revealed that the pistol belonged to one of David's close friends, a man who lived in a large, fancy house just north of Preston Center in Dallas, near where David had his medical offices.

"Sandra was very close with this man's wife," Leake explained. "I know from multiple witnesses Sandra was always hanging around over at the house. The ladies both loved champagne; they would hang around at the pool and drink champagne into the evening."

The pistol, Leake discovered, was known to be kept in a dresser in the back house apartment over the garage of this friend's home. "I do not believe that David went into the back house apartment over the garage and stole the pistol," Leake stated firmly. "I believe the totality of circumstances indicates that she did."

In the aftermath of David's death, Sandra's behavior raised eyebrows among those who knew her. Despite having just lost the father of her three children, Sandra displayed what many perceived as a surprisingly cheerful demeanor. Even more puzzling to those around her was her apparent lack of sentimentality regarding the mementos of her late husband and their life together.

"When Sandra sold David's dental practice to a female dentist in Dallas," Leake recounted, "the new dentist told Sandra, 'Kathy Giddings' portraits of your three beautiful children are here. They're beautiful. Come by and get them any time.' The dentist thought it was notable that Sandra never came by to get the photos."

This seeming indifference to family photographs that most would consider priceless keepsakes was just one of many behaviors that struck those who knew Sandra as odd or unsettling in the wake of her husband's death.

But if David's death marked the end of one chapter in Sandra's life, it also opened the door to new opportunities for social advancement. With her first husband barely in the ground, Sandra wasted no time in setting her sights on bigger prizes in Dallas society.

A New Target in Dallas High Society

A year after burying her first husband, whose suspicious death with a handgun was ruled a suicide, Sandra struck up a relationship with a very wealthy high profile restauranteur.

This new relationship marked a significant step up the social ladder for Sandra and demonstrated her remarkable ability to insinuate herself into the highest echelons of Dallas society. The man in question was none other than Norman Brinker, a figure whose influence on American dining culture cannot be overstated.

"Norman Brinker was a famous entrepreneur," Leake explained, his voice tinged with a mixture of admiration for Brinker's accomplishments and concern over his entanglement with Sandra. "He was an Olympic equestrian. I believe it was the 1952 Olympics in Seoul, Korea. A real man's man, handsome, rich."

Brinker's claim to fame extended far beyond his athletic prowess or personal wealth. He was, as Leake put it, "famous for starting this whole new style of dining in the United States." Brinker pioneered what would come to be known as "casual dining" - a category that fell somewhere between fast food and formal restaurants.

"It's somewhere between fast food and really formal," Leake elaborated. "They call it casual dining. There's a categorical name for these casual dining chains that are affordable for middle-class families, but you nevertheless took your family and sat down and had proper service."

Brinker's innovations in this arena were numerous and far-reaching. "Steak and Ale was an early Norman Brinker venture," Leake noted. "And then ultimately, he was involved in Chili's, TGI Fridays, you know, multiple casual dining chains. He made a great fortune. Norman Brinker is really one of the great restaurateurs of all time in terms of his portfolio."

It was into this world of wealth, innovation, and high-stakes business that Sandra managed to insert herself. The meeting between Sandra and Norman Brinker seemed, on the surface, to be a chance encounter. "Sandra encountered Norman at a car wash," Leake recounted. "As he perceived it then, it was a fortuitous encounter. He found her very charming."

Brinker, apparently captivated by Sandra's beauty and charm, invited her out on a date. What followed was a brief but high-profile romance that saw Sandra and Norman spotted about town together, firmly establishing her presence in Dallas's social elite.

However, Sandra's relationship with Norman Brinker was not destined to last. Whether Brinker saw through Sandra's facade or simply lost interest is unclear, but the brief romance ended, leaving Sandra once again on the hunt for a wealthy partner who could provide the lifestyle to which she aspired.

Wealth, Death, and Manipulation

With her sights set firmly on climbing even higher up the social ladder, Sandra began to employ increasingly brazen tactics to pursue wealthy men. Her hunting grounds expanded to include not just social functions and chance encounters but even religious institutions.

"Church, specifically an Episcopal Church, became a focal point for Sandra's pursuits," Leake revealed. He went on to describe a particularly shocking incident involving a church leader, though he was careful to protect the identity of the family involved.

"She did seduce a churchwarden, a married man, a very wealthy man," Leake said, his tone grave. "She was able to extract - how to put it - well, I'll just jump to it. She persuaded him to cosign a loan."

The details of this incident, as Leake uncovered them, paint a disturbing picture of Sandra's manipulative abilities. The churchwarden, Leake explained, thought he was merely guaranteeing the loan so that Sandra could obtain it and service it herself. However, Sandra had no intention of paying a penny towards the loan.

When the lenders sued the churchwarden for non-performance of the loan, he responded with a cross-action suit against Sandra. It was at this point that Sandra revealed her true nature and the extent of her manipulation.

"As she began to speak, with the court reporter typing away, about the details of their intimate relationship," Leake recounted, "his attorney waived the whole thing off and said, 'We'll settle the matter. Let's just forget it. We'll petition the court to dismiss this with prejudice.'"

This incident marked a turning point in Sandra's tactics. As Leake observed, "It's an interesting moment in Sandra's career because she realized if you're a married man, and you're a high-profile guy, and particularly if your public image is that of a churchwarden, you are going to take great pains to avoid exposure."

Sandra had discovered a powerful tool for manipulation - the threat of scandal and public humiliation. It was a tool she would wield with devastating effect in the future.

Throughout my conversations with John Leake, one question kept surfacing: What was it about Sandra that made her so alluring? How was she able to captivate so many successful, ostensibly intelligent men?

Leake, who had encountered Sandra multiple times in his early teenage years while living down the street from her, provided a vivid description of her appeal. "Even as a 13 and 14-year-old boy," he recalled, "I remember this smoldering presence. At the time, I didn't know what I was looking at. But 13, 14 - it's a time of awakening sexuality. I remember even then thinking, 'There's something mesmerizing about this woman.'"

He went on to describe Sandra's physical attributes in detail: "She had these big brown eyes that would just hold you in her gaze, and whatever you were saying, I was probably talking about a BMX bike or something - she would hold you with this gaze as though it was the most fascinating thing she'd ever heard."

But it wasn't just her attentive gaze that men found captivating. "She had this lustrous brown hair," Leake continued. "And what I remember, and what other men have admired, was this white skin, this milky white skin that contrasted with her raven hair and brown eyes."

The overall effect, according to Leake, was nothing short of devastating. "She was devastating," he emphasized. "Particularly if you were a man who had not had this kind of attention from a woman like that for a long time, if ever."

Sandra's ability to make men feel special, to give them her undivided attention and make them believe they were the most fascinating person in the world, was a powerful tool in her arsenal. Combined with her striking looks, it made for a nearly irresistible package - one that would prove fatal for some of the men who fell under her spell.

As our conversation continued, I pressed Leake for more details about Sandra's methods. How did she manage to insert herself into the lives of so many wealthy, high-profile men?

"Sandra was incredibly skilled at putting herself in the right place at the right time," Leake explained. "She had an uncanny ability to show up where wealthy, influential men would be. Whether at church functions, charity galas, or even in their offices - Sandra found a way to be there."

Leake went on to describe how Sandra would use her physical presence to her advantage. "She had this way of touching men on the arm as she spoke to them," he said. "It was a subtle gesture but incredibly effective. It created an immediate sense of intimacy, of connection."

But it wasn't just her physical tactics that made Sandra so effective. She was also a master of conversation and manipulation. "Sandra had done her homework," Leake noted. "She knew about art, about fine wines, about interior design. She could speak intelligently on a wide range of topics that interested wealthy men. And more importantly, she knew how to listen."

This ability to be the perfect audience, to make men feel heard and understood, was perhaps Sandra's most potent weapon. "She had this way of making you feel like you were the only person in the room," Leake said. "Like everything you said was incredibly important and fascinating to her. For men who were used to being surrounded by people who wanted something from them, this kind of attention was intoxicating."

As Leake delved deeper into Sandra's background and methods, a picture emerged of a woman who had honed her skills of seduction and manipulation to a fine art. She was not just beautiful but intelligent, charming, and incredibly perceptive. She knew how to read people, how to give them exactly what they wanted - or what they didn't even know they wanted.

"Sandra was like a chameleon," Leake observed. "She could be whoever she needed to be to get what she wanted. With some men, she played the role of the sophisticated socialite. With others, she was the damsel in distress, in need of rescuing. She had an uncanny ability to figure out what each man needed and become that person."

This chameleon-like quality extended beyond her personality. Sandra was also skilled at adapting her appearance to suit her targets. "She knew how to dress, how to carry herself," Leake explained. "Whether she needed to look elegant and sophisticated or young and vulnerable, Sandra could pull it off convincingly."

However, perhaps the most chilling aspect of Sandra's methods was her apparent lack of empathy or genuine emotion. "Despite her ability to charm and seduce, there was always something cold about Sandra," Leake said. "People who knew her well often commented on how she could switch her emotions on and off like a faucet. One moment, she'd be laughing and charming, and in the next moment, she'd be ice cold."

Within a year of her husband's death, Bridewell hunted for a new suitor.

A whirlwind romance and marriage to her second husband catapulted her to the top of Dallas society---but not for long.

In the opulent world of 1970s Dallas high society, few figures shone as brightly as Bobby Bridewell. As true crime author John Leake explains, "It's no exaggeration to say Bobby Bridewell was the most popular man in Dallas society. Everybody loved Bobby."

Leake paints a vivid picture of a man larger than life, brimming with charisma and an infectious zest for living. "He had this infectious humor and lust for life and having a good time," Leake recounts. Bobby's charm was matched only by his business acumen and social connections. Coming from a Tyler, Texas, oil family, he had transitioned from the oil business into hotel development, a move that would prove pivotal in his rise to prominence.

"He was friends with Eric Hilton. He was friends with the Sands family, the Hunt family," Leake explains, emphasizing the extent of Bobby's social and business network. These connections weren't just social niceties; they were the backbone of his success in the hotel industry. Bobby's crowning achievement, as Leake puts it, was "developing the Mansion on Turtle Creek. That's kind of his crowning achievement as a hotel developer."

The Mansion on Turtle Creek wasn't just another hotel; it was a statement of luxury and prestige in Dallas. Robert Riggs, the interviewer, underscores its significance: "Any Hollywood celebrity comes to Dallas. This is where they stay or anybody that's high profile with money." The hotel's development was a testament to Bobby's vision and his ability to transform the old into something spectacularly new.

Leake delves into the history of the property, explaining its transformation from a cotton baron's mansion to a luxury hotel. "Shepherd King was a cotton Baron. You know the old saying in Texas before oil, cotton was king," he notes. The mansion, built in the 1920s, symbolized the wealth generated by the cotton industry in Dallas. "Shepard King made a fortune in cotton, and he wanted to build the most stately home in all of Dallas. So he brought in masons from Italy, and he built this mansion on Turtle Creek in the 1920s," Leake recounts.

By the late 1970s, when Bobby Bridewell set his sights on the property, it had fallen into disrepair. "By the time Bobby starts eyeballing this, it's basically abandoned," Leake says. But where others saw decay, Bobby saw potential. "He has this vision. This could be a luxury hotel, kind of like the Hilton Hacienda in Santa Fe," Leake explains. Bobby's plan was ambitious: to preserve the original mansion while adding a modern hotel in the same architectural style, creating a haven for the rich and famous visiting Dallas.

Bobby's vision for the Mansion on Turtle Creek came to fruition through a fortuitous connection. Leake reveals, "Bobby Bridewell's friendship with one of the sons of Texas oil heir Caroline Rose Hunt turned the Mansion into the first luxury property of the Rosewood Hotels and Resorts." This connection was no small matter. Caroline Hunt, as Leake points out, "became one of the nation's wealthiest women in the 1980s, turning a $600 million dollar inheritance into vast wealth north of a billion dollars by the time of her death in 2018."

The Hunt family's wealth and influence were legendary. Caroline's father, H.L. Hunt, was a storied wildcatter who had amassed an incredible fortune. Leake notes that H.L. Hunt was "perhaps the world's richest man when he died in 1974." This context underscores the magnitude of Bobby's achievement in partnering with the Hunt family for the Mansion on Turtle Creek project.

215

The success of the Mansion on Turtle Creek solidified Bobby's status as a key player in Dallas society. For Sandra Bridewell, marrying Bobby was "the catch of all catches." She had aligned herself with one of the most charismatic and well-connected men in Dallas, a move that would catapult her into the upper echelons of society.

However, Bobby's life wasn't all business success and social triumph. Leake reveals a more personal side of Bobby's story, one that would eventually lead to his fateful meeting with Sandra. "Bobby owned a thoroughbred racehorse farm and training track in Celina, about 40 miles north of Dallas," Leake says. This extravagant hobby was, as Leake puts it, "just an outrageous extravagance, for I mean, he did well in the hotel business, but to have a thoroughbred breeding facility in Celina, Texas, just north of Dallas was quite something."

Before Sandra entered the picture, Bobby was married to "a beautiful Southern Belle from Virginia." But this marriage would end in heartbreak and humiliation for Bobby. "The story is that he caught her in flagrante delicto with her horse trainer," Leake reveals. "It was kind of a blow to his heart and ego. He loved this girl. It was a little bit of a, you know, a rude awakening for him."

This personal setback left Bobby in an unusually vulnerable state. "So he, for the first time in anyone's memory, Bobby was rather despondent," Leake explains. It was in this context that Bobby's friend, Beau Price, decided to intervene. With Bobby's 37th birthday approaching, Price had an idea to lift his friend's spirits – and he knew just the woman for the job.

Enter Sandra Stegall, recently widowed after her first husband's alleged suicide. Beau Price saw an opportunity to introduce Sandra to Bobby at his birthday party. The introduction was far from subtle. "At the climactic moment, she jumped out of a cake," Leake recounts, painting a vivid picture of Sandra's dramatic entrance into Bobby's life.

The effect was immediate. When asked if Bobby was immediately smitten, Leake confirms, "He's immediately charmed by this girl." The attraction was so strong that Bobby quickly moved to end his marriage. "Quickly goes ahead and moves forward with a divorce from his wife. The ink is hardly dried on the divorce decree when he marries Sandra a month later," Leake explains.

This whirlwind romance marked a significant turning point in Sandra's life, elevating her status in Dallas society. Leake, who lived in the same neighborhood as the newlyweds, provides a firsthand account of this period. "Bobby and Sandra bought a house on Lorraine Avenue in Highland Park. I grew up on Lorraine. So she and her three children from her first marriage and Bobby buy a house just down the street from me," he recalls.

The marriage, while brief, was by all accounts a happy one. "It was by all accounts a fun marriage with prosperity because he was developing the mansion on Turtle Creek," Leake says. However, the joy was short-lived. Bobby was diagnosed with lymphoma, a diagnosis that would prove terminal.

During their brief marriage, from 1978 to 1982, Sandra enjoyed a meteoric rise in Dallas society. "Sandra was something of a socialite," Leake notes. "She was invited to these parties and the Cattlemen's Ball. I think she was actually part of the Committee on that. She was something of a lady about town."

However, as Bobby's health declined, a new and pivotal relationship began to form in Sandra's life. Robert Riggs points out, "And when he is suffering from cancer, she becomes very close with his oncologist and the wife of his oncologist." This relationship with Dr. John Bagwell and his wife, Betsy, would be a critical turning point in Sandra's story.

Leake elaborates on this development: "By the time you get to end of 1981, early 1982, it's become evident that Bobby is a goner. I mean, it's very aggressive chemotherapy. You know, he's basically skin and bones lost all of his hair, he's very sick." As Bobby's condition worsened, Sandra seemed to become increasingly dependent on the Bagwells. "She seems to become more and more dependent needy, in terms of calling on requesting assistance from the oncologist not only as a treating physician for Bobby, but, you know, a general seeking help and assistance from the oncologist family," Leake explains.

The Bagwells were not just any family in Highland Park. Dr. John Bagwell came from a line of prominent physicians. "Dr. John Bagwell was the son of a very prominent physician in Dallas. Father was also John Spurgeon Bagwell. Bagwell was the president of staff at the Baylor University Medical Center, a very prominent Dallas physician," Leake notes. The younger Bagwell had followed in his father's footsteps, becoming "the oncologist of Highland Park society."

Living in a beautiful house on Maplewood Avenue, in what Leake describes as "the heart of old Highland Park," the Bagwells represented another level of Dallas society that Sandra seemed to aspire to. "Sandra, it would seem began to think of Dr. Bagwell began to fantasize about Dr. Bagwell as a very interesting man with a very interesting position in society," Leake surmises.

Another Death Under Suspicion

However, this growing connection between Sandra and the Bagwells would soon take a dark turn. Just two months after Bobby Bridewell succumbed to cancer, a shocking event occurred that would forever change the lives of all involved.

On what seemed like an ordinary day, Betsy Bagwell was contacted by Sandra. The story, as relayed to the Dallas Police, was that Sandra's car had broken down at the Highland Park Presbyterian Church. She asked Betsy for a ride to the rent-a-car agency at Love Field Airport. This simple request would be the last time anyone saw Betsy Bagwell alive.

Leake recounts the tragic turn of events: "Betsy was last seen with Sandra in Betsy's car so Betsy herself is giving Sandra a ride to Love Field airport, purportedly to rent a car a few hours later. Betsy is found shot to death in her car parked in the short-term parking lot at Love Field."

The circumstances surrounding Betsy's death were immediately suspicious. Sandra Bridewell was the last person to see her alive, a fact that would become increasingly significant as more details emerged. When asked about Sandra's alibi and the crime scene, Leake provides a detailed account of the events and subsequent investigation.

"The timeline of this is pretty, pretty intriguing," Leake begins. He recounts how Betsy had lunch with her two best friends at the Dallas Country Club just before meeting Sandra. During this lunch, Betsy expressed frustration with Sandra's constant presence in her life. "Sandra is driving me nuts," Betsy reportedly told her friends. "You know, I felt bad when her when Bobby died. I understand she has to rear three children on her own. But she keeps showing up all the time. She keeps saying her cars breaking down the lady is driving me nuts."

Despite her apparent annoyance, Betsy agreed to give Sandra a ride to Love Field. This decision would prove fatal. Betsy never returned home from this errand, even though she was in the midst of preparing dinner. Her disappearance initially went unnoticed, and it was only through a strange twist of fate that her body was discovered.

Leake describes the bizarre circumstances of the discovery: "Some children look into the car. It's this brand new Mercedes 300 TT wagon. The father of the children is a Mercedes mechanic. And as he's pulling into a field, he tells the children that is the most beautiful family car ever built. That sparks the curiosity of the children that look into the vehicle. And they see this woman stretched all the way out across the seats of the vehicle, her head and her upper body are actually lying on the passenger seat of the vehicle."

When the Dallas police arrived at the scene, it initially appeared to be a suicide. Betsy was found with a revolver in her right hand. However, Leake's investigation years later would reveal troubling inconsistencies in this initial assessment. "It's clearly braced between her right thigh and the gear shifter. In a way that looks very staged," he notes.

The weapon itself raised questions. It was a cheap 22-caliber revolver, the same type infamously used by John Hinckley in his assassination attempt on President Reagan. More importantly, the gun was stolen and traced back to a man who had died years earlier. The question of how Betsy would have obtained this weapon was never satisfactorily answered.

Sandra's actions following Betsy's death added another layer of suspicion to the case. She was dining with friends at a restaurant called Le Tosca when Dr. Bagwell called, asking about Betsy's whereabouts. Sandra's explanation to Dr. Bagwell was convoluted and inconsistent with her later statements to the police.

When the police informed Dr. Bagwell of his wife's death, Sandra arrived at the Bagwell house shortly after. In her statement to the police, she painted a picture of Betsy as a troubled woman interested in suicide. "Sandra tells the cop at least what's noted in the reports, and they're very, very cursory reports. Sandra tells the cop I spent the day with Betsy; she seemed despondent. She wanted to talk about a nurse at her husband's hospital. And she really wanted to ask me about the circumstances of my first husband's suicide."

This statement contradicted what Betsy had told her friends at lunch earlier that day. Those friends, who never spoke to the police, were convinced that Sandra had murdered Betsy. "They had no doubt at the time that Sandra had murdered Betsy. But they never went to the police to share their perceptions, their suspicion or their conviction," Leake reveals.

When asked about Sandra's potential motive for murder, Leake presents a compelling theory. "Sandra told a woman with whom she was close at the time that she was having an affair with Dr. Bagwell," he explains. "She told her, her civil attorney who was Bobby Bridewell's attorney before he died, she told him that she was having an affair with Dr. Bagwell."

Leake posits that Sandra believed that if Betsy were found dead of an apparent suicide, it would deepen her relationship with Dr. Bagwell. "She would in effect, supplant Betsy and her home and as the partner of Dr. Bagwell," he suggests. However, this plan, if it existed, backfired spectacularly.

Dr. Bagwell, despite the official ruling of suicide, seemed to suspect foul play. "He didn't care what the police or the medical examiner were saying Sandra murdered her," Leake states. However, Dr. Bagwell found himself in a difficult position, unable to challenge the official findings without revealing the complex dynamics of his relationship with Sandra.

Leake's investigation, years later, would uncover evidence that supported the theory of foul play. "I believe that if Dr. Bagwell had at the time, the police were looking at this given a full and candid account of this fraught relationship with Sandra, they would have viewed this with far graver suspicion," he concludes.

The aftermath of Betsy's death created a stark divide between what the Dallas Police knew and what Highland Park society believed. "There's like this Great Wall of China insulation between what the Dallas Police know and what Highland Park society knows or thinks it knows," Leake explains. This resulted in Sandra being ostracized from the social circles she had worked so hard to enter.

An Obsessive Pursuit of Wealth

Despite the swirling rumors and suspicions, Sandra found a new romantic interest. In June of 1984, two years after Betsy's death, she met Alan Rehrig, a young man who had just arrived in Dallas from Edmond, Oklahoma. Their meeting seemed like a chance encounter, with Alan looking for a place to stay and Sandra watering her azalea bushes.

Their romance was swift and intense. "Whirlwind romance ensues," Leake describes. "She tells him a few months later she's pregnant. He proposes marriage. He's a Christian boy from Edmond, Oklahoma, who wants to do the honorable thing and proposes marriage." They married in December of 1984, but their happiness was short-lived. A month after the wedding, Sandra told Alan she had miscarried.

What Alan didn't know was that the entire pregnancy had been a ruse. "Unbeknownst to Alan, he never learned this. She'd actually had a hysterectomy years earlier. So the whole pregnancy was fraudulent," Leake reveals. Despite this deception, Sandra convinced Alan to purchase a life insurance policy with a $220,000 death benefit.

Six months later, the couple separated. On the eve of their first wedding anniversary, Alan Rehrig told a friend he was going to run an errand with Sandra.

A few days later, Rehrig was found shot to death in his parked car near the Oklahoma City airport, a three-hour drive away from Dallas.

Leake says Sandra told Oklahoma City homicide detectives that her estranged husband was hanging around with gambling bookies, and she suspected of him having an addiction to cocaine.

Meanwhile, Gloria Rehrig, his mother, received an anonymous phone call telling her about the suspicious deaths of Sandra's first husband and Betsy Bagwell.

Gloria Rehrig petitioned a court to stop paying her late son's life insurance benefits to Sandra Bridewell and removed her as the administrator of her son's estate.

Alan Rehrig's first cousin replaced Bridewell, and a few days later, he was found shot to death in his car parked inside the garage of his home.

The cause of death was ruled a suicide.

Under a cloud of controversy stemming from her connection to three gunshot deaths, Sandra Bridewell suddenly bolted out of Dallas in 1986.

The mysterious circumstances surrounding Alan Rehrig's death sent shockwaves through the community and raised alarming questions about Sandra Bridewell's involvement. As Leake delves deeper into the case, he uncovers a web of deceit and manipulation that seems to follow Sandra wherever she goes.

A Chilling Pattern of Deception

"Sandra's statement to the Oklahoma City homicide detectives is particularly interesting," Leake explains. "She paints a picture of Alan as a man involved with unsavory characters - gambling bookies - and suggests he had a cocaine addiction. This narrative seems designed to deflect suspicion away from herself and onto these shadowy figures from Alan's alleged secret life."

However, those who knew Alan found these claims hard to believe. Friends and family described him as a straight-laced, Christian young man from Oklahoma with no known history of drug use or gambling. The discrepancy between Sandra's portrayal and the Alan known to his loved ones deepened the mystery surrounding his death.

The anonymous phone call to Gloria Rehrig, Alan's mother, proved to be a pivotal moment in the case. "This call was like a bolt from the blue," Leake says. "Suddenly, Gloria was confronted with the possibility that her son's death wasn't an isolated incident, but potentially part of a pattern involving Sandra Bridewell."

The information about the suspicious deaths of Sandra's first husband and Betsy Bagwell cast a long shadow over Sandra's innocence. It prompted Gloria to take decisive action to protect her son's estate and legacy.

"Gloria's petition to the court was a bold move," Leake notes. "It shows a mother's determination to seek justice for her son, even in the face of powerful opposition. By stopping the life insurance payout and removing Sandra as the administrator of Alan's estate, Gloria effectively cut off Sandra's financial gain from Alan's death."

This legal maneuver set off a chain of events that would lead to yet another tragedy. The appointment of Alan's first cousin as the new administrator of the estate appeared to be a prudent choice - a family member who could be trusted to handle Alan's affairs with care and respect.

"The death of Alan's cousin ruled a suicide, adds another layer of complexity to this already convoluted case," Leake observes. "The timing - just days after replacing Sandra as the estate administrator - is highly suspicious. It raises the question: was this really a suicide, or was it another calculated move to maintain control over Alan's estate?"

The official ruling of suicide in the cousin's death echoes the initial determination in Betsy Bagwell's case. In both instances, the circumstances surrounding the deaths raised more questions than they answered, leaving family members and investigators alike grappling with doubts and suspicions.

West Coast Reinvention

As the cloud of controversy grew thicker around Sandra Bridewell, her sudden departure from Dallas in 1986 seemed to confirm the suspicions of many. "Sandra's decision to leave Dallas so abruptly is telling," Leake argues. "It suggests a woman who felt the walls closing in, who recognized that her carefully constructed facade was crumbling under the weight of mounting suspicion and scrutiny."

The timing of her departure, linked to her connection to three gunshot deaths, painted a picture of a woman fleeing from her past. However, as Leake discovered in his investigation, Sandra Bridewell's story was far from over.

"Sandra's exit from Dallas marks the end of one chapter in her life, but it's really just the beginning of a new one," Leake explains. "Her move to the West Coast opens up a whole new arena for her particular brand of charm and manipulation."

Indeed, as Leake would uncover in his trailing of Bridewell to the West Coast, Sandra's pattern of behavior seemed to continue, albeit in new and unexpected ways. The tale of romance scams and identity theft that would unfold in the coming years would add yet another dimension to the already complex portrait of Sandra Bridewell.

"What's fascinating about Sandra's move to the West Coast is how she seems to reinvent herself," Leake observes. "Yet, at the core, her methods remain the same. The charm, the manipulation, the ability to insinuate herself into people's lives - these traits persist, just in a new environment."

The Master Manipulator's New Persona

The story of Sandra Bridewell on the West Coast would prove to be a masterclass in deception and reinvention. From affluent suburbs to religious communities, Sandra seemed to have an uncanny ability to identify and exploit vulnerabilities in those around her.

"One of the most striking aspects of Sandra's West Coast period is her use of religion as a tool," Leake notes. "She often presented herself as a devout Christian woman, using this persona to gain trust and sympathy from church communities. It's a stark contrast to her life in Dallas, yet it proved equally effective in opening doors and creating opportunities for her."

As Leake delved deeper into Sandra's activities on the West Coast, he uncovered a series of romantic entanglements and financial schemes that left a trail of broken hearts and empty bank accounts. "Sandra's modus operandi on the West Coast was remarkably consistent," Leake explains. "She would often target wealthy, often older men, presenting herself as a woman in need of help or protection. Her ability to adapt her story to appeal to each new target was truly remarkable."

One of the most alarming aspects of Sandra's West Coast activities was her propensity for identity theft. "Sandra didn't just steal hearts and money," Leake reveals. "She stole entire identities. We found instances where she had assumed the identities of other women, using their credit histories and personal information to further her own ends. It's a level of deception that goes beyond simple fraud - it's a complete erasure and replacement of another person's existence."

The scope and sophistication of Sandra's schemes on the West Coast paint a picture of a woman who had honed her skills of manipulation and deception to a fine art. From elaborate backstories to forged documents, Sandra seemed always one step ahead of those who might expose her true nature.

"What's particularly chilling about Sandra's West Coast period," Leake observes, "is how she seemed to learn from her experiences in Dallas. She became more careful, more nuanced in her approach. The overt connections to mysterious deaths that had marked her time in Dallas were replaced by a subtler form of exploitation. It's as if she had refined her methods, becoming even more dangerous in her ability to manipulate and deceive."

As Leake's investigation would reveal, Sandra's time on the West Coast was marked by a series of narrow escapes and near-misses. Time and again, she would be on the verge of exposure, only to slip away and resurface elsewhere, often with a new identity and a new set of victims.

"The pattern that emerges from Sandra's West Coast activities is one of constant movement and reinvention," Leake explains. "She never stayed in one place for too long, never allowed people to get too close or to start asking too many questions. It was a nomadic existence, but one that allowed her to stay ahead of her past and continue her schemes."

The tale of Sandra Bridewell on the West Coast is more than just a story of crime and deception. It's a study in the psychology of a master manipulator, a woman who seemed to have an almost preternatural ability to read people and situations.

In May 1987, *D Magazine*, the glossy monthly publication that chronicles Dallas society and gossip, published a cover story that would change the trajectory of Bridewell's life.

"*D magazine* did a cover story on the Black Widow," Leake explains, his voice carrying a mix of fascination and gravity. "By then, she'd been given that moniker - the Black Widow. That D magazine cover story, which was published a year after Sandra left Dallas, was an absolute sensation."

The impact of this story cannot be overstated. In today's world of instant information and viral content, it's hard to imagine the slow burn of scandal in the pre-internet age. Yet, the story of Sandra Bridewell managed to captivate and horrify readers, spreading through more traditional means.

The story would have gone viral, but this was the pre-internet age.

But someone started pumping out copies of the story on their fax machine to wherever Sandra Bridewell showed up in the Bay Area of California.

Leake paints a vivid picture of Bridewell's new stomping grounds. "Belvedere is an upscale, affluent community just on the north side of the Golden Gate," he describes. "The San Francisco Yacht Club is in Belvedere, on the north side of the Golden Gate. Sandra had taken up residence in Belvedere, in an apartment next door to the Yacht Club. She'd ingratiated herself with this affluent society in Marin County."

But Bridewell's attempts to start anew were thwarted by her past catching up with her. "These D Magazine copies start showing up at the homes and offices of prominent people," Leake continues. "And the signal is clear: Be very, very careful with this lady."

Despite the warnings, Bridewell managed to continue her modus operandi. Leake reveals, "She's gotten back into borrowing money from married men." When pressed about the amounts, Leake provides startling figures. "One guy said she'd gotten about $30,000 out of him. The other guy, she'd gotten $76,000 out of him. And they claimed that she asked for this money as a loan."

Leake goes on to describe Bridewell's manipulative tactics. "After they loaned her the money, she said, 'Well, thank you for your generosity. I think I'll be moving on my merry way.' And when the men said, 'Well, no, wait a minute. What are you talking about? That was a loan,' she said, 'I don't know what you're talking about. Why don't you discuss this with your wife?'"

The audacity of Bridewell's actions is clear in Leake's retelling. "These two guys concluded they didn't want to be pushed around like this. So they told their wives what had happened. The wives forgave them, let's say, or decided that they were going to stand by their husbands even though their husbands had made these indiscreet decisions with Sandra."

Leake emphasizes the significance of these incidents. "Those were two civil cases that added to the fact pattern. This is what she does. She befriends married men, she borrows money from them, and then she doesn't pay them back." He adds, with a note of certainty, "I believe those two guys that came forward are just the tip of the iceberg."

As Bridewell's schemes began to unravel in the Bay Area, she once again took flight. Leake describes this period as her "wandering spirit" phase. "She becomes a wanderer, a drifter," he explains. "She leaves the Bay Area. She turns up in Tucson, Arizona."

The story of Sandra Bridewell might have faded into obscurity at this point, were it not for the persistent efforts of investigative journalist Glenna Whitley. Leake credits Whitley's work for keeping tabs on Bridewell's movements. "Now we're getting into this era of Sandra wandering around, but with a kind of heightened awareness," he says. "Glenna starts getting calls from people from different parts of the country saying, 'I've encountered this woman.'"

Bridewell's nomadic lifestyle took her back to California, where she settled for a time in Palo Alto, in the heart of Silicon Valley. But it was in the early 1990s that Bridewell's persona underwent another dramatic transformation.

"She seduces a married man in the Bay Area," Leake recounts. "She claims she's pregnant. He is trying to figure out a way to manage this with his wife." The situation led to an unusual arrangement. "His wife says, 'Well, okay, you've severed the relationship with her. But you know, I don't trust that you'll stay away from her.' So the arrangement he makes with Sandra is he moves her to Boston. And he rents an apartment on Boston's Beacon Hill. That's the arrangement - she's going to be on the other side of the country."

It was at this juncture that Bridewell, now in her early 50s, began to show a renewed interest in religion. Leake notes, "She develops an interest in the Christian religion. Now, she'd already demonstrated an early interest in this when she was a member of the Highland Park Presbyterian church congregation. But now she really gets into it."

This religious awakening wasn't just a passing phase. "She actually received some ministerial training," Leake explains, "and starts introducing herself as a minister. And as a missionary. And this is a whole other chapter in the story of

231

Sandra's adventures as an apparent ministering Christian missionary."

Bridewell's new persona as a missionary opened up new avenues for her to exploit. Leake describes how she would present herself to unsuspecting strangers: "People would occasionally encounter Sandra on an aircraft, you know, in an airport, just random encounters in a coffee shop, wherever, and she proclaimed to be a Christian missionary in the United States, in between missions."

Her stories were elaborate and designed to impress. "She claimed she was often in Africa or India, or in the Third World, doing the work of the Lord as a missionary, looking after the needy, the undernourished," Leake continues. "Like Christ Himself, tending to the sick and the poor. And people found this very compelling. And she knew the Bible very well."

It was during this period that Bridewell, now going by the name Camille (her mother's first name), met her fourth husband at a church conference in Colorado. Leake provides insight into the man who would become Bridewell's next victim: "I think that he was a man that was genuinely seeking spiritual renewal. His first marriage had not worked out."

The man had attended what Leake describes as "the Wagner ministerial training institution" in Colorado Springs. "He's doing this sort of ministerial apostolic training at this institute. And he meets this woman who introduces herself as Camille."

Leake's description of the man's initial impression of Bridewell is telling: "He's genuinely moved by her apparent embrace of the Holy Spirit. I mean, her knowledge of the New Testament, particularly, is just astonishing. And she seems to be, as he perceived her, sort of burning with the Spirit of God."

The whirlwind romance quickly led to marriage. But as Leake recounts, the facade quickly crumbled: "The way he describes it, as soon as they married - I mean on their wedding night - she seems to undergo a radical change. The sort of sweet Christian lady turns into, very quickly, what he perceived to be, in his own words, 'like a witch.'"

The man found himself in a nightmare scenario. "He quickly comes to wit's end," Leake explains. "She's taken out a bunch of credit cards in his name. She's never there. She's doing all of this traveling to tony resorts and spending all of his money and steals his gold coin collection, steals his car. I mean, he just doesn't know what hit him."

What makes this story particularly tragic, Leake notes, is the man's complete ignorance of Bridewell's past. "He had traveled to Colorado Springs from San Antonio. His home is San Antonio, Texas. He's never heard anything about this woman. So it's a huge shock to him to discover, you know, you're not this lady's first rodeo."

The financial damage was substantial. Leake confirms, "She sticks him with $150,000, I think, charges on his credit card. And he was very proud of his gold coin collection. She took that along with his Ford Explorer, and none of that property was ever seen again."

As Bridewell continued her travels, she had another significant encounter on a flight. Still using the name Camille, she claimed to be returning from an overseas mission. Leake picks up the story: "She lands in San Francisco. It's funny, she oftentimes circles back to the Bay Area."

On this particular flight, Bridewell sat next to a woman from Santa Rosa, just north of Marin County. Leake recounts the conversation, "Sandra is talking to the lady. She says, 'I'm headed back to San Francisco after my last mission.' And the lady says, 'Well, where do you live?' And Sandra says, 'Oh, really, I'm on my way to Santa Rosa. But as it turns out, I don't have a place to stay. I'm meeting with some people in Santa Rosa, but I haven't yet organized accommodation.'"

This chance encounter led to Bridewell's next scheme. "That quickly lands her in a church congregation in Santa Rosa," Leake explains. "She meets an elderly man, he's really at the end of his life. He's on dialysis. I mean, he's not in good shape."

Bridewell saw an opportunity and seized it. "Sandra makes the case that she could be a caretaker of this elderly man," Leake continues. "His wife, who's initially grateful for the home care, quickly realizes something strange about this woman. She seems to be trying to ingratiate herself with the infirm husband, who has an estate and who's at the end of his life."

The situation quickly deteriorated. "That turns into a rupture with the elderly man's wife. But by then, he's already been pretty charmed by Sandra," Leake says. The conflict escalated to the point where law enforcement became involved. "The Santa Rosa sheriff's department gets involved. They report Sandra to protective services or some sort of Adult Protective agency. And they tell her, 'You're gonna have to back off from this family.'"

While Bridewell wasn't arrested, the incident marked an important moment in terms of law enforcement awareness. Leake reveals, "A sheriff's deputy writes an incident report saying law enforcement should keep an eye on this lady. He says, 'I don't think she's a minister or missionary. I think that she is a con artist who seeks elderly people with an estate in order to ingratiate herself and to obtain access to the estate.'"

Following this incident, Bridewell once again disappeared. Leake picked up her trail a few years later: "She turns up again, a few years later in North Carolina. She's introducing herself to elderly people as Camille Bowers. So now she's really changed her name." And she resembles a bag lady.

Leake's description of Bridewell at this point in her life is striking. "Her circumstances have obviously diminished considerably from when she was a socialite in Highland Park," he observes. "She looks very thin, but in a kind of fascinating way it almost adds to her saintly appearance. She almost looks like an ascetic saint."

Scams and Identity Theft in North Carolina

Despite her diminished circumstances, Bridewell's ability to manipulate people remained intact. "People observe she seems to be carrying around sort of tattered bags and a worn-out old suitcase," Leake continues. "But she says, 'I'm a Christian missionary, and I'm in between missions to Africa. And I could use a place to stay in the interim.'"

It was with this persona that Bridewell ingratiated herself with an elderly lady in Southport, North Carolina, a woman named Sue Moseley.

Moseley was an affluent elderly lady who lived alone and had health problems. The Good Samaritan took in Bridewell, who professed to be an itinerant minister and missionary who liberally quoted the Bible chapter and verse.

Bridewell, who used the alias Camille Powers, helped with the shopping and cooking. Once she won Moseley's trust, she stole her identity.

Bridewell got caught trying to transfer Moseley's monthly social security check to her bank account.

Jayne Todd, a North Carolina Sheriff's detective who investigated case said Bridewell was a psychopath who moved in on the elderly Ms. Moseley like a predator.

The detective said quote, "All that business about being a good Christian and a missionary tending to the needy of the world. That was just a lie. No doubt she was the evilest person I've ever encountered."

In 2007, Sandra Bridwell finally had a day of reckoning with the criminal justice system for the elderly Ms. Moseley.

While awaiting trial on federal charges of aggravated identity theft, John Leake interviewed Bridewell behind bars.

Leake's encounter with Bridewell in prison provides a fascinating glimpse into her character and demeanor after years of deception and manipulation. "The voluptuous, smoldering femme fatale had been replaced by a slightly gaunt-looking woman," Leake recalls. Her demeanor was very dignified. She had this erect posture, and she made direct eye contact."

Despite the years and circumstances, Bridewell still managed to project an air of mystery and intrigue. "She had this dignity about her, which I found... I couldn't quite put my finger on it, but I found it very interesting," Leake muses. However, he quickly realized that getting information from Bridewell would be challenging. "Clearly, she either through her own wits or her attorney, you know, had been told not to talk to anybody about any of this. I could not get her to tell me anything."

Bridewell, aka Sandra Camille Powers, pleaded guilty to federal charges of aggravated identity theft in 2008. She served two years in a federal prison.

While behind bars, she became a prison pen pal with a North Carolina minister.

Even from behind bars, Bridewell's ability to charm and manipulate remained intact. Leake explains the unusual situation that developed: "A church minister or pastor in a rural county of North Carolina, for some reason, has taken a fancy to Camille Powers, as he keeps calling her."

The minister's interest in Bridewell led to an unexpected arrangement. "He persuades the prison system that upon being released from her federal sentence, he will look after her," Leake continues. "She can work for his church and his charity during her probationary period where she has to remain in North Carolina."

A Chameleon's Last Transformation

However, true to form, Bridewell's behavior quickly raised red flags. Leake recounts a particularly telling incident: "She then charges a very large Victoria's Secret lingerie purchase on the pastor's credit card." The situation was so embarrassing for the pastor that he was reluctant to take official action. "He told the sheriff's deputy, but he stopped short of filing a formal report with a statement," Leake explains.

In the wake of the federal identity theft conviction, Oklahoma City prosecutors reopened the homicide investigation of Alan Rehrig, Bridewell's third husband.

The grand jury declined to indict her.

Bridewell then turned up in Vermont, offering to bail a farmer out of financial trouble by purchasing his herd of fleece-bearing Alpacas.

Leake picks up the story of Bridewell's latest scheme in Vermont. "She says she's interested in purchasing his alpaca herd," he explains. "She says that she has experience in animal husbandry because her first husband was a thoroughbred racehorse breeder. And she likes rural living, likes living on a farm, likes animals."

The farmer, intrigued by Bridewell's offer, was swept up in her charm. "She answers the Craigslist ad, and a whirlwind romance ensues," Leake recounts. "And it's yet another saga in this story."

However, as had happened so many times before, the farmer began to doubt Bridewell. "He, like others in the internet age, begins to think, 'Well, there's something odd about this woman,'" Leake explains. "He does a Google search for her alias, and he gets this hit, and he realizes she's done time in a federal pen in North Carolina. And the story unfolds from there."

But Bridewell, ever resourceful in her deceptions, had one more trick up her sleeve. Leake reveals, "She tells him she's pregnant." This claim, outlandish as it might seem, was a tactic Bridewell had used before. "Now, he doesn't know her age," Leake continues. "He assumes her to be in her 50s. She still looks like an attractive woman. But nevertheless, his parents are both doctors. He thinks she's too old to get pregnant."

The reality of Bridewell's age makes her claim even more absurd. "Unbeknownst to him, at the time she claims to be pregnant, she's actually in her late 60s. I think she's 66,"

Leake says. "So later, upon discovering her true age, he realizes that that's a rather absurd claim."

The Vermont farmer cut off the relationship, and Sandra Bridewell faded away.

There was a recent sighting of her at the Boston Logan Airport.

Lingering Mysteries and FBI Suspicions

Leake obtained a heavily censored FBI report that raises questions if Bridewell had allegedly been involved in cocaine smuggling, international arms trafficking, and with an accomplice in the murder of her third husband.

The FBI report Leake mentions adds yet another layer of intrigue to Bridewell's already complex story. While heavily redacted, the document hints at potential involvement in serious criminal activities that go far beyond romance scams and identity theft. If true, the implications of cocaine smuggling and international arms trafficking would elevate Bridewell from a local con artist to a player in global criminal networks.

Moreover, the suggestion of an accomplice in the murder of her third husband reopens questions about Alan Rehrig's death. While a grand jury declined to indict Bridewell, the FBI report suggests that law enforcement may have had lingering suspicions about her involvement.

These allegations, while unproven, paint a picture of a woman whose criminal activities may have been far more extensive and dangerous than previously known. The contrast between the glamorous Dallas socialite and the potential international criminal is stark, highlighting the enigmatic nature of Sandra Bridewell's character.

239

A Legacy of Deception and Darkness

As of 2024, Sandra Bridewell, once a celebrated Dallas socialite, is 80 years old and continues to be a figure shrouded in mystery and intrigue. A woman of many faces—murder suspect, seductress, romance scammer, saintly missionary, and convicted identity thief—she endures in the public imagination as a mysterious princess of darkness.

The story of Sandra Bridewell is a testament to the complex and often baffling nature of human behavior. From her beginnings as a celebrated socialite in Dallas's elite Highland Park community to her later years as a convicted felon and suspected international criminal, Bridewell's life trajectory reads like a work of fiction.

Yet, it's the very real consequences of her actions that make her story so compelling and disturbing. The trail of broken marriages, financial ruin, and shattered trust she left in her wake speaks to a pattern of behavior that goes beyond simple opportunism or greed.

Bridewell's ability to reinvent herself time and again—as a grieving widow, a devout missionary, and a savvy businesswoman—suggests a chameleon-like adaptability that allowed her to prey on the vulnerabilities of those around her.

The moniker "Black Widow" given to her by the Dallas media is particularly apt, not just because of the suspicious deaths surrounding her but also because of her apparent ability to ensnare her victims in a web of deceit. From wealthy businessmen to elderly retirees, from church pastors to struggling farmers, Bridewell seemed to have an uncanny ability to identify and exploit the weaknesses of others.

Perhaps most intriguing about Bridewell's story is the question of motivation. Was she driven by a pathological need for attention and admiration? Was it pure greed? Or was there something more profound, more complex at play? The fact that she continued her schemes well into her senior years, long past the point where one might expect such behavior to taper off, suggests a compulsion that goes beyond simple material gain.

The heavily redacted FBI report mentioned by Leake adds another layer of mystery to Bridewell's story. The suggestions of involvement in international crime rings - cocaine smuggling and arms trafficking - if true, would elevate Bridewell from a local con artist to a figure of global criminal significance. It also raises questions about how much of her activity over the years may have gone undetected or unreported.

The reopening of the investigation into Alan Rehrig's death, Bridewell's third husband, is particularly noteworthy. While she was never formally charged with his murder, the lingering suspicions and the mention of a possible accomplice in the FBI report suggest that there may be more to this case than initially met the eye. It's a stark reminder that behind the salacious headlines and fascinating psychological profile, there are real victims whose lives were irrevocably altered by their encounters with Sandra Bridewell.

As Bridewell enters her ninth decade, her story serves as a cautionary tale about the dangers of charm divorced from conscience, of religiosity without true faith, of the masks people wear, and the lengths some will go to maintain their facades. It's a story that challenges our assumptions about class, gender, and age - reminding us that predators can come in many forms, even those we least expect.

The fact that there was a recent sighting of Bridewell at Boston Logan Airport suggests that even at 80, she may not be done writing her story. One can't help but wonder if she's still running cons, still reinventing herself, still searching for that next mark. Or perhaps, in her twilight years, she's finally found some measure of peace or reflection on her tumultuous life.

In the end, Sandra Bridewell remains an enigma - a woman who, despite years of scrutiny and investigation, still manages to elude full understanding. Her story is a testament to the complexity of human nature, the power of deception, and the sometimes fine line between charm and manipulation.

She endures in the public imagination as a "mysterious princess of darkness" - a figure who continues to fascinate and repel in equal measure. Her legacy serves as a reminder of the potential for darkness that exists within human nature, and the devastating consequences when that darkness is allowed to flourish unchecked.

The story of Sandra Bridewell is more than just a true crime tale or a sensationalized account of a femme fatale. It's a complex narrative that touches on issues of identity, morality, and the human capacity for both deception and belief. It raises uncomfortable questions about how well we can ever truly know another person, and about the masks we all wear in our daily lives.

For those who encountered Bridewell throughout her life - her husbands, her victims, the law enforcement officers who pursued her - she represents a pivotal moment, a brush with a force of nature that left an indelible mark. For the rest of us, her story is a fascinating case study in the psychology of deception and the enduring power of charisma, even when wielded for nefarious purposes.

Ultimately, the story of Sandra Bridewell - the Black Widow of Highland Park - reminds us of the complexity of human nature, the power of narrative, and the thin line that sometimes separates truth from fiction in the stories we tell about ourselves and others. It's a story that will likely continue to captivate and unsettle us for years to come, a dark fairy tale for our modern age that reminds us that, sometimes, the most dangerous predators are the ones hiding in plain sight.

Robert Riggs

Hard Time in Hell: Among Texas' Most Dangerous Prisoners

The Texas prison system, one of the largest in the world, is a place few can fully comprehend unless they've lived or worked within its razor-wire confines. It is defined by hardened criminals, intricate power dynamics, and a history steeped in violence and reform. Former warden David Stacks, with 30 years of firsthand experience, offers a glimpse into this harsh, self-contained world where survival often depends on strength, wit, and, sometimes, brutality.

David Stacks Warden Texas Eastham Prison Unit 2003

"When I say these guys were bad," Stacks reflects, "I mean it. They were the kind of people you wouldn't want to meet in a dark alley. Tough isn't even the word—it goes beyond that. They were dangerous in a way that seeps into everything around them."

Today, Stacks directs the Texas Prison Museum in Huntsville, preserving the history and artifacts of Texas's complex prison system. The museum's centerpiece, an electric chair known as "Old Sparky," serves as a symbol of a dark legacy while reminding visitors of the state's enduring stance on punishment.

The Funeral Director's Fall from Grace

The story of the Texas prison system includes some of the most colorful characters—and horrifying stories. Stacks recalled a particular inmate who once ran a respectable funeral business in East Texas. "He had three funeral homes, as I recall, and he knew how to talk to people. But he got greedy," Stacks says.

The man used his pilot's license to fly to Mexico, trafficking marijuana to expand his wealth. Eventually, his marriage soured, and his wife threatened to turn him in. Desperate, he decided to eliminate the threat. "He killed her," Stacks recounts, "put her body in a tub and used chemicals he knew would dissolve it. And down the drain, she went."

This was no spur-of-the-moment decision; it was calculated, something that seemed almost detached, according to Stacks. "I asked him how he got caught," Stacks says, "and he shrugged. 'I got drunk at a bar and bragged to someone sitting next to me," he told me.

It was chilling. A man so careful brought himself down by loose lips. This kind of story was not uncommon in the prison system, where high intelligence and desperation often crossed paths, leading to bizarre and dark consequences.

The Ramsey Unit: Where the Past Meets the Present

Many Texas prisons have histories that stretch back to the 1800s, standing on grounds once worked by enslaved people or, later, convict laborers. The Ramsey Unit, where Stacks once worked, is one such place. Set on land that was once a series of plantations, the prison's layout and work programs echo a long and troubled past. Inmates tend to cattle, pick crops, and maintain the grounds under the blazing Texas sun—conditions that recall a time when the line between freedom and incarceration was even more blurred.

It was here that Stacks witnessed one of the more creative escape attempts of his career. A prisoner facing a new 75-year sentence simply could not accept the future that lay before him. "He couldn't face it," Stacks explains. "But because of his record, he was given a job in the shower area." The bus that brought inmates in and out of the unit would park near the showers, allowing a brief and risky opportunity. Over time, the man collected a long wooden plank left near the showers and attached it to the bus chassis. "He rolled out beneath the bus, undetected," Stacks recounts, "making his way through three separate units. No one questioned it, and it would've worked—if someone had been doing their job."

The Retrieve Unit: The Inferno for Hardened Criminals

The Retrieve Unit, now known as the Scott Unit, was notorious for its population of hardened criminals. The prison once held Kenneth Allen McDuff, a convicted serial killer whose story remains one of the most infamous in Texas history. "But McDuff wasn't even the worst we had," Stacks says. "He was nothing compared to some of the others."

McDuff's presence might have been notorious, but within the prison walls, it held little significance. "Some guys at Retrieve had been on Death Row and had their sentences commuted to life," Stacks explains. "These were the kind of men you never fully trusted, even if they acted reformed. There was one guy I remember who was responsible for running the boiler room. He could blow the whole prison up if he wanted to. But he did his job and had no issues. These guys—whether you call it respect or fear—knew they had to make their life work here."

Retrieve was known for more than its notorious inmates; it was a place where violence simmered just below the surface. Fights rarely ended in mere bruises. "Most altercations involved knives," Stacks recalls. "There was this gang hit that comes to mind—the Pistoleros targeting a Nuestra Familia member. It wasn't a brawl; it was calculated and planned. And it ended in death. Violence at Retrieve was a part of daily life."

The Challenges and Dangers of a Corrections Officer's Life

Few jobs are as hazardous and psychologically taxing as that of a corrections officer in Texas. The dangers officers face are always present, but some days bring tragedy. Shortly before Stacks' interview, 27-year-old corrections officer Jovian Motley lost his life attempting to restrain an inmate at the Eastham Unit. The facility, once home to notorious prisoners and legendary escape attempts, remains as dangerous today as ever. Motley's death raised questions about safety protocols and, critically, staffing shortages.

"Our officers are stretched thin," Stacks admits. "It's not an easy job. There are days when you wonder if you'll make it home." Stacks reflects on his experience, contrasting it with the perils facing modern law enforcement. "Walking down those halls, I never had to worry about a gun being drawn on me. But for law enforcement today, every traffic stop is potentially fatal. They have no idea what they're walking into."

Calculated Minds and the Art of Manipulation

Prison might appear as a world dominated by brute force, but intelligence and cunning often hold equal weight. Stacks encountered numerous inmates who possessed not only sharp minds but also the patience and skill to exploit any oversight to their advantage.

"There's a misconception that prisoners are just violent thugs," Stacks says. "The reality is that many of them are intelligent, highly observant, and patient. That's what makes them dangerous." One incident involved a high-ranking member of the Texas Syndicate prison gang, who came to a unit for medical treatment. The inmate asked Stacks's Major to place his brother in solitary confinement for protection. "He told us he'd been ordered to kill his brother," Stacks recalls. "He didn't want to do it, but he knew he'd be expected to report back to his gang. So, we put the brother in isolation. If we hadn't, I have no doubt he would've gone through with it. It was calculated, detached."

The 5 Percent Problem

As Stacks describes it, the Texas prison system is marked by a rule of averages: 95% of inmates adjust, work within the system, and adhere to structure. "But that last 5%—they're the ones who keep the rest of us on edge," he says. These individuals, he explains, are beyond rehabilitation, driven by a violent or sociopathic nature. "There's something in them that doesn't fit anywhere. They aren't simply victims of circumstance—they're just evil."

The prison population was surprisingly productive when held within strict boundaries, Stacks explains. "For many, it's the absence of drugs and alcohol that calms them down. They work, they follow orders, and they find a routine. But if you took away that structure, I have no doubt some of them would revert." Stacks compares it to classroom dynamics, where one disruptive child can ruin the experience for everyone else. "Most prisoners know how to 'do time,'" he says. "But those few who can't—or won't—are always watching for ways to disrupt the system."

Preserving Texas Prison History

Today, Stacks runs the Texas Prison Museum, an institution that offers a sobering look at the complex history of the Texas penal system. One of the main exhibits is "Old Sparky," the electric chair used from 1924 to 1964. "We tell people the truth here," Stacks says. "There's no sugarcoating it. The convict leasing system, for example, was one of the cruelest, most mismanaged programs in Texas history. It's something we never want to repeat."

The museum has attracted a unique visitor demographic: former inmates, many of whom come with their children. "They're showing their kids the life they left behind," Stacks says. "For some, it's a chance to scare their kids straight. For others, it's about confronting their past."

Some former inmates are humbled by the experience, Stacks notes, while others bring an air of bravado. "They act tough like it was all a walk in the park," he says, "but when they see what's here, that attitude changes. And then some still carry a hint of that gang mentality, coming in with their girlfriends, showing off. We welcome them all the same as long as they behave."

A Lasting Legacy of Caution and Reflection

Texas has always been a place of contradictions, and the prison system reflects this complexity. For Stacks, the years have left him with an understanding that not every story is simple. "Most inmates, in my view, just lost their way somewhere along the line," he says. "But then there are those who you realize are dangerous.

An FBI Agents Relentless Pursuit Of A Dallas Drug Kingpin. It's A Case Of Pure Evil.

A Ruthless Drug Lord

Geno Ruiz Camacho was a ruthless drug king in Dallas, Texas, during the late 1980s.

Connected to a powerful Mexican drug cartel, Camacho had an insatiable lust for violence.

Fellow drug dealers noted that he could turn his brutality on and off like a light switch.

A Crime Scene of Unimaginable Horror

Camacho once told his right-hand man that he planned to "cut out a guy's heart and eat it and make him eat it too.

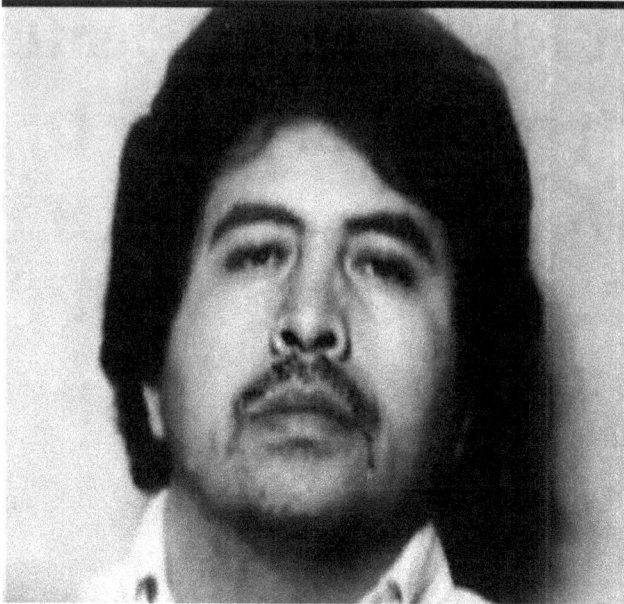

Geno Camacho FBI Wanted Poster

During his capital murder trial, a prosecutor described Camacho as a "mad dog killer." After jurors sentenced him to death, the judge remarked that the trial had featured "the most grotesque and bizarre set of facts ever heard in a courtroom in this nation since the Charles Manson killings in California," He called the verdict "exceedingly appropriate."

Just how grotesque, you wonder? Camacho put a woman through a tree mulcher and murdered a four-year-old boy and his mother.

The Man Behind the Badge

FBI Special Agent Tase Bailey of the Dallas Violent Crime Task Force pursued Camacho for two years. At the time of the trial, Bailey said Camacho was the worst criminal he had encountered in 21 years.

In 2024, long retired from the Bureau, Bailey sat down to talk to me about the case that still haunts him today.

We had a history together from my reporting years earlier on bank robbery takeover gangs and wanted violent fugitives.

Reporter Robert Riggs Receives The Dallas Crime Commission's Inaugural Excellence in Reporting Award From US Attorney Paul Coggins and FBI Agent Tase Bailey

In 1999, Bailey presented me with the first-ever Dallas Crime Commission Award for "Excellence In Crime Reporting."

Tase Bailey joined the FBI after serving with the Marines in Vietnam.

After 14 years with the Bureau, Bailey transferred to the Dallas Field Office to head up the Dallas SWAT team and work violent crime cases.

The violent crime squad covered everything from bank robberies, kidnappings, extortions, armored car robberies, and fugitives. They hunted fugitives wanted for murder, armed robbery, kidnapping, and other violent crimes in Texas.

The Brutal Beginning

The Camacho case began with a brutal murder and kidnapping at a crack house in Pleasant Grove, a notoriously violent neighborhood in southeast Dallas. To this day, Pleasant Grove remains a hotspot for crime.

On the day in question, 33-year-old Geno Camacho arrived outside the house with three accomplices. Camacho, a stocky and swarthy 5-foot-7, 175-pound drug dealer, was already wanted in South Texas for killing a man with a shotgun over a trivial name-calling dispute. His presence exuded a sinister aura reminiscent of an evil 19th-century ghost.

Camacho parked his car in front of the dilapidated two-story crack house. He psyched himself up for the confrontation by banging his fists on the steering wheel. He had fronted $30,000 worth of marijuana to 31-year-old Evelyn Banks, an occasional drug dealer who lived there with her 3-year-old son, Andre, and her common-law husband, 52-year-old Sam Junior Wright. Wright, the boy's father, was also a wanted fugitive drug dealer.

It was time for Evelyn to pay the piper.

Wright had tried to sell the drugs at housing projects, but she had been ripped off and couldn't pay Camacho for the stolen drugs.

Camacho kept calling for his money. Banks ignored his calls and would not answer the door to her home.

So Camacho finally got fed up.

Camacho rounded up some muscle to assist him in collecting his debt.

He and Juan Jackson, his girlfriend's 24-year-old brother, headed to Eddie Blaine Cummings's two-bedroom apartment.

Cummings, a muscular 24-year-old known as "Fast Eddie," had been Camacho's cellmate in the Dallas County Jail a few months earlier. He already had a long rap sheet, including narcotics violations, illegal possession of firearms, and stealing several thousand dollars from his mother.

Camacho burst into the apartment, shouting, "Wake up! We got work to do!" But Cummings, who was in bed with his 23-year-old girlfriend, Pamela Miller, was sleeping off a hangover. The night before, Cummings and Camacho partied and got drunk at Baby Dolls, a strip club where Pamela Miller worked as a topless dancer.

Groggy and irritable, Cummings refused to budge. He told Camacho to round up his roommate, George David Cooke, and 38-year-old Larry Gene Merrell, known as "The Indian," to help with the job.

When Camacho arrived at the house, he found it secured with burglar bars on all the windows. The bars on the front door were wrapped with a chain and padlocked.

Camacho sent Juan Jackson to cut the telephone line from the side of the house. They then cut the chain on the front door and kicked it in. David Cooke was armed with a .357 handgun, while either Juan or Larry Merrill wielded a MAC-10 submachine gun. Once inside, they grabbed Evelyn and sent one of the men upstairs to fetch Sam Wright and Andre Banks, Evelyn's three-year-old son, and brought them downstairs.

Camacho began screaming for his money, demanding immediate payment. David Wilburn, Sam Wright's nephew, arrived at the house during this chaotic moment. They were planning to travel to Shreveport for a funeral that day, and Sam, a federal fugitive on drug charges, did not want to drive for fear of being arrested. Wilburn, who had a clean record, was supposed to drive.

The Execution

The intruders brought Wilburn inside, forced him to his knees, and made him lie flat on the floor. Camacho, determined to show he meant business, ordered David Cooke to shoot Wilburn in the head. When Cooke hesitated, Camacho took the gun and shot Wilburn himself.

With the immediate threat dealt with, Camacho grabbed Sam, Evelyn, and Andre and marched them out to a Lincoln Continental, which belonged to David Cooke's mother. As they got into the car, Sam Wright desperately ran for it. Camacho sent Juan after him, but he couldn't catch Sam. Camacho and his men took Evelyn and Andre to an apartment at Royal and Central, leaving Evelyn with Cooke, Eddie Blaine Cummings, and Larry Merrill. Realizing the gravity of the situation, Merrill left, saying, "I'm getting out of here."

Camacho took his hostages, Evelyn Bailey and her three-year-old son Andre, to the apartment where Fast Eddie Cummings lived with his topless dancer girlfriend Pamela Miller. Fast Eddie held the mother and child there for two days. Pamela Miller realized she was witnessing a crime that she should not see.

Breaking News

FBI Special Agent Tase Bailey watched the television news coverage of the murder and kidnapping while sitting in the hospital, where his daughter was recovering from a tonsillectomy.

Bailey sensed immediately that drug traffickers were involved. He said that Dallas had so many kidnappings that you could tell by the neighborhood crime patterns that this was not a sex-related kidnapping. It was a kidnapping to collect a drug debt.

Sam Wright, the fugitive drug dealer who had escaped, called the FBI and informed them that Camacho had taken Evelyn Banks and her son Andre hostage over the $30,000 she owed him for 25 pounds of marijuana.

Authorities were unaware that the mother and child were being held at the apartment of Eddie Blaine Cummings, "Fast Eddie," with his girlfriend, Pamela Miller, the stripper.

In the meantime, FBI Special Agent Bailey tracked down Camacho's wife, Vicki.

Camacho's wife told Agent Bailey that her husband had a girlfriend named Wanda Jackson. Wanda lived in Richardson, a northern suburb of Dallas. Jackson had a striking look because she wore contact lenses to make her eyes look blue. Camacho's wife told the FBI she was trying to get a divorce from Camacho, but he threatened all of her lawyers. So, no one would represent her in the divorce case because they feared Camacho. She wanted a divorce because she had caught Camacho molesting their daughter. The FBI ran a background check on Wanda Jackon, and Bailey interviewed her. Wanda Jackson claimed she had not seen Camacho in over a week because she was at a funeral. However, the FBI later found out that when they left, Jackson called Camacho to warn him that the FBI was looking for him. She said, "Big brother's been here. And he says you've been a very bad boy." That spooked Camacho.

The FBI quickly identified Camacho and his three accomplices.

The Trail Turns Cold

But the trail had gone cold by the end of the first week.

Camacho had made no effort to contact anyone to demand ransom for Evelyn Banks and her three-year-old son, Andre. There were no clues about the location of the kidnapped victims or Camacho's whereabouts.

A new lead emerged when Pamela Miller, the topless dancer and girlfriend of Fast Eddie Cummings, was reported missing.

A friend informed the police that Miller had mentioned witnessing "something she shouldn't have" and that she was planning to go away for a while.

Another acquaintance recognized Camacho from newspaper stories as the man she had seen with the stripper and others at Baby Dolls topless club.

The FBI received the first of two significant breaks three months into the investigation. A snitch reported that Fast Eddie Cummings was hiding in his hometown of Lawton, Oklahoma, and planned to visit a restaurant. U.S. Marshals apprehended him and served him dessert in handcuffs.

Cummings unraveled the story of the murder and abduction, revealing the involvement of David Cooke, who had hesitated to pull the trigger to kill David Wilburn. Cooke agreed to plead guilty to one federal count of kidnapping in exchange for sharing what he knew.

The Abduction

What he revealed was horrifying. Two days after the murder, an enraged Camacho informed Cooke that his girlfriend, Wanda Jackson, had just been interviewed by FBI Agent Tase Bailey. Furious that the FBI was closing in on him, Camacho ordered Cooke to snatch Evelyn Banks and her son Andre from the apartment shared with Fast Eddie Cummings.

Camacho then directed Cooke to find 26-year-old Spencer Stanley, a dangerous psychopath who did his dirty work. The group transported Banks and her son north to Ardmore, Oklahoma, just across the border from Texas. Cooke recounted how Camacho kept Banks calm by telling her they were flying her to California from a clandestine airstrip.

They traveled to Ardmore, Oklahoma, and checked into a motel room. Camacho instructed Spencer Stanley to find a place to dispose of Evelyn and Andre, though he did not say this in their presence. Familiar with the area, Stanley ventured out to a remote location, drove along backroads into the woods, and dug a long, deep hole. He returned to the hotel and informed Camacho that he had finished digging the makeshift grave.

The following day, Camacho told Evelyn they were going to a clandestine landing strip in the woods, where a plane would take them to California. He assured her they would stay in California until the situation cooled down, and then they could return. They drove to the remote area along a dirt road and walked into the woods. As soon as Evelyn saw the hole, she realized their fate. She let out a scream and collapsed. Stanley, who had Andre on his shoulders, threw the little boy into the hole. Camacho then fired four rounds from a .380 handgun into Andre's body, killing the three-year-old. He pushed Evelyn into the hole and shot her multiple times. They covered the bodies with cat litter before filling the hole and concealing it with brush. Afterward, they drove to a boat ramp on Lake Texoma in Tishomingo and threw the .380 murder weapon into the lake.

After two days of bumping along the back roads of southern Oklahoma, David Cooke finally located the remote grave site of Evelyn Banks and her son, Andre.

The Gruesome Discovery

On a sweltering August afternoon in Oklahoma, with no breeze to offer relief, FBI agents began their grim task of digging. They soon uncovered spent .380-caliber cartridges, a chilling testament to the violence that had occurred. After two hours of labor, an FBI agent, standing waist-deep in the hole, unearthed the remains.

A foul stench filled the air, overwhelming the agents. They neutralized the odor by smearing Vicks VapoRub under their noses. As they continued to dig, they found Evelyn lying as she had died on top of her son. Both bodies were partially mummified by the cat litter the killers had spread over them.

Another grisly revelation awaited. En route from Dallas to search for Banks and her son, David Cooke, in a matter-of-fact tone, made a startling disclosure about the disappearance of Pamela Miller, the topless dancer from Baby Dolls.

David Cooke recounted the grim events as Bailey and fellow FBI Agents drove him up Interstate 35 from Texas to Oklahoma. Agent Bailey knew Pamela Miller was missing and that she had witnessed something at the apartment, she shouldn't have seen. Bailey asked Cooke about her and mentioned that the FBI had heard that Camacho had taken her to Mexico. Cooke was evasive, and the FBI agent kept pressing Cooke for an answer.

Bailey asked, "Where's Pamela Miller now? Where in Mexico is she?" Cooke replied, "She's not in Mexico; she's dead." Bailey then inquired where she was buried, to which Cooke chillingly responded, "You'll never find her." When Bailey demanded to know why, Cooke revealed, "We ran her through a tree milcher."

Upon hearing this revelation, Bailey recalled nearly running off the road as Cooke continued to detail Camacho's growing paranoia about Pamela Miller.

Camacho had taken Pamela with him to a drug deal because she had seen too much. They went to an Irving, Texas, hotel near the DFW airport. Camacho was trying to arrange a big drug deal because he needed money to flee to Mexico. He met a man interested in buying drugs at the Anatole Hotel in Dallas. Camacho, David Cooke, and the violent psychopath Spencer Stanley brought Pamela Miller along. During the meeting, Pamela, who had been drinking heavily, told the drug dealer that she recognized him as a regular to the Baby Dolls strip club, where she danced. Miller's familiarity with his identity made the potential drug buyer nervous, and he excused himself to use the restroom, then slipped out the back door, never returning. The busted drug deal infuriated Camacho, who dragged Pamela out to the car and began punching her. Her derogatory comments about his masculinity only enraged him further.

In the backseat of the car, Camacho began strangling Pamela. Believing she was dead, he moved to the front seat, but Stanley observed, "Geno, I think she's still alive." They pulled her out of the car, slammed her on the side of the road, and drove the car over her. Stanley noted again, "I think she's still alive." They drove further, then ran her over once more. Eventually, they reached Stephenville, where David Cooke had an apartment. They placed her body in a barrel and left her there for a couple of days.

Cooke then called his friend, Steve Smith, instructing him to rent a tree mulcher and bring it to Stephenville. When Smith arrived, Camacho and his accomplices hauled the barrel that contained Pamela Miller's body to Cooke's family's ranch in a remote area of Stephenville located west of Fort Worth. They dumped Pamela's body out of the barrel, and Spencer Stanley used an axe to cut up the young woman's body parts as they fed her remains into the true mulcher.

FBI Agent Bailey escorted Cooke to his mother's ranch, where she willingly consented to a search of the property.

Bailey recalled the grizzly scene in which they found pieces of bone chips with notches that had clearly been through a grinder.

Two days later, a team of FBI agents returned to the scene. They divided an area half the size of a football field into a 20-foot-square grid. Agents used grass clippers and trowels to dig through the grass for bone chips. It had not rained, so pieces of tissue from Pamela Miller's body were still hanging in the trees. Agents found a jawbone with teeth still intact, which helped identify Miller.

Bailey successfully apprehended all of Camacho's accomplices. It was a motley crew, particularly David Cooke, the criminal who struck a deal with prosecutors to expose the full extent of the crimes.

David Cooke had purchased the Mac10 submachine gun used in the kidnapping. FBI Agent Bailey said Cooke was a sadistic person who liked to torture animals. A brutal story circulated that Cooke had buried a litter of kittens up to their neck and ran over them with a lawn mower.

Spencer Stanley was an uncontrollable, hyper-psychopath. Fast Eddie Cummings was just a punk, according to Bailey. Larry Merrill, who was present during the kidnapping, hung out with crews to supply his drug habit. Bailey says Merrill left once he realized what was going on.

FBI Special Agent Tase Bailey discovered that Camacho had raped a woman in South Texas before fleeing to southwestern Mexico.

Camacho was hiding out in Arecelia, where his girlfriend's brother was a member of a drug cartel.

Today, the state of Guerrero, where Arecelia is located, has a reputation as the most brutal and heinous crime state in the recent history of Mexico.

Forty-three young students disappeared here in 2014.

Arcelia is a strategic zone for illicit trade—minerals, weapons, drugs, and human trafficking.

When the FBI wanted to capture Camacho, the Mexican government refused to help.

According to Bailey, it declared it would require military action to take Camacho into custody, effectively rendering him untouchable.

Meanwhile, Dallas County Sheriff's intelligence agents intercepted a letter from Camacho to a Jamaican drug dealer soliciting a hit on David Cooke. Cooke was in the same jail as the Jamaican. You may recall it was Cooke who cooperated with the FBI, leading them to the grave where Camacho killed the mother and her child and the site where he disposed of the topless dancer's body in a tree mulcher.

Luring Camacho Across the Border

Determined to bring Camacho back, Bailey devised several schemes to lure the violent killer across the border into the United States.

A breakthrough came when a DEA informant managed to entrap Camacho. The informant boasted about his connections with mob figures in Kansas City and mentioned that organized crime associates were interested in purchasing 10 tons of marijuana. At the time, marijuana's wholesale price on the border was about $300 a pound, making it a potential $6 million deal.

Anticipating that Camacho would verify the informant's credibility, Bailey contacted one of his confidential sources within the Mexican drug trade. He alerted the source that Camacho might call for verification. When Camacho did, Bailey's source reassured him that he was dealing with legitimate contacts.

Bailey's source reinforced the informant's credibility by emphasizing his connections and financial backing. Despite the setup, Camacho still hesitated to cross the border. To sweeten the deal, the informant offered Camacho $100,000 in earnest money, which he could only collect in person by crossing the Rio Grande River into McAllen, Texas. Camacho took the bait.

The DEA informant convinced Camacho to cross the border posing as a tourist, carrying a bottle of tequila, intending to meet the informant and the drug dealer at a hotel in McAllen.

To ensure recognition by the FBI, the informant gave him a distinct outfit: white shorts, turquoise blue and white Cole Haan loafers, a Hawaiian shirt, and a matching blue and white hat with the phrase "Beauty is skin deep, but ugly goes to the bone."

Bailey still laughs about the gaudy outfit that Camacho agreed to wear.

As Camacho crossed the bridge, FBI and DEA agents, disguised in plain clothes, were strategically positioned. Soon, a DEA agent radioed, "He's on the bridge now." Bailey requested confirmation, "Are you sure it's him?" The agent replied, "Yes, he's wearing those goofy clothes the informant gave him."

As soon as he crossed the bridge, the agents closed in. They pretended to be Border Patrol, telling him they suspected he was an illegal immigrant and asked for his identification. Camacho replied, "I don't have my ID. I just went across to get a bottle of tequila. Here it is. My name is Tomas Sanchez." The agents responded, "We think you're an illegal immigrant, and we need to take your prints to verify your citizenship."

They took Camacho to the Border Patrol office and placed him in a lockup. At this point, Bailey's blood pressure was pumping in anticipation of arresting Camacho.

Bailey waited about two or three hours to avoid making it obvious that Camacho had been set up so he would not compromise the DEA informant. After this deliberate delay, Bailey walked into the cellblock with his fingerprint cards and introduced himself, saying, "Tomas, I'm Tase Bailey from the FBI. I think you know who I am."

Camacho replied, "No, I don't know. I've never heard of you." Despite his denial, Bailey knew that his girlfriend Wanda had tipped him off that Bailey was on his trail after the kidnapping. Bailey continued, "Well, your fingerprints came back, and they identify you as Geno Camacho." Bailey then showed him his mug shot and said, "And that's you, right?"

Camacho reluctantly replied, "I guess so. The fingerprints must be right." Bailey informed him, "I have a warrant for your arrest for murder and kidnapping." His response was terse, "Well, it must be."

The FBI Agent concluded the interview, saying, "We're taking you back to Dallas." Camacho simply said, "I don't have anything to say." Bailey nodded and said, "Okay."

On the flight back to Dallas, the small single-engine, six-seat FBI aircraft hit turbulence.

Bailey had been rattling Camacho by staring him down.

When the plane started bouncing around the sky, Camacho nervously asked, "Are we going to die?"

The pilot turned around with a grin and replied, "No, we are not, but you are."

The Trial and Justice

Camacho stood trial for the murder of David Wilburn in a Dallas County Criminal Court before the U.S. Attorney would prosecute him for kidnapping Evelyn Banks and her son.

The FBI agent expected Camacho would get the death penalty in state court. Bailey said that trying him first in state court and then in federal court was, in effect, an insurance policy. If Camacho's death penalty sentence were overturned on appeal, it would ensure that the brutal drug kingpin would spend the rest of his life in federal prison.

In the spring of 1990, a Dallas County jury sentenced Geno Camacho to death for the execution-style murder of David Wilburn two years earlier. Wilburn had tragically shown up at the wrong place at the wrong time, interrupting the abduction of Evelyn Banks and her three-year-old son, Andre.

During the two-week trial, held under maximum security, the jury heard harrowing testimony about Camacho's brutal crimes. They learned how he had murdered Pamela Miller and fed her body into a tree mulcher and how he had ordered the execution of Evelyn Banks and her young son.

"Why did the 3-year-old have to die?" prosecutor Hugh Lucas asked the juror before turning to look directly at Camacho. "He wasn't going to be an eyewitness to anything." Addressing the jury, Lucas continued, "You, at this point, become the conscience of the community."

Lucas called Camacho "the baddest of the bad, the meanest of the mean." He asserted, "If this death penalty was ever warranted, this is the case."

Several jurors sat crying after more than four hours of deliberation, visibly shaken, as District Judge Ron Chapman read their verdict. The 35-year-old Camacho showed no emotion. He made the sign of the cross as sheriff's deputies escorted him out of the courtroom.

There were fears that the cartel might attempt to help Camacho escape. So, Sheriff's deputies put him in a bright orange jumpsuit to be visible. They handcuffed him and drove him straight to an airstrip in a heavily armed motorcade.

A Texas Department of Public Safety aircraft transported Camacho straight to Texas Death Row in Huntsville, Texas, to await execution.

Tase Bailey and the FBI continued hunting Camacho's accomplice, Juan Jackson.

The television show Unsolved Mysteries aired a segment about the fugitive, leading to a breakthrough.

The manager of a soft drink bottling company in Compton, California, recognized Jackson as an employee loading trucks at his plant.

Co-workers knew him as "Country" for his thick Texas accent and notified the FBI.

FBI agents quickly moved in and apprehended Jackson, bringing him back to Dallas to stand trial in federal court.

Jackson and Camacho were tried and convicted of kidnapping Evelyn Banks and her three-year-old son, Andre.

This conviction served as an insurance policy, ensuring that Camacho would spend the rest of his life behind bars if his death penalty sentence were ever overturned.

The Final Chapter in the Texas Death Chamber

In late August 1998, exactly ten years to the day since Tase Bailey and fellow FBI agents exhumed the bodies of Evelyn and Andre Banks, Camacho faced the Texas executioner.

Bailey, his former boss on the violent crimes squad Joe Hersley, and Pamela Miller's mother, Mickey Miller, were present inside the Huntsville Walls Unit's Death Chamber.

Mickey Miller, the mother of the dancer who Camacho had fed into a tree mulcher, pressed herself against the glass window of the booth reserved for victims' families.

Camacho lay on a gurney with his arms outstretched and intravenous tubes inserted.

Ms. Miller chanted, "You're paying. You are finally paying."

Bailey muttered under his breath, "Suck it up, Mr. Badass. You're going to be dead in about five minutes."

The warden asked Camacho if he had any last words. Camacho looked at his family, who were witnessing the execution in the room next to Millers. He said, "I will see you on the other side."

As the deadly chemicals started flowing into Camacho's body, family members began pounding on the glass window of their room.

Within a few minutes, Camacho started to snore, stopped breathing, and was pronounced dead.

Bailey thinks Camacho got off easy in comparison to the pain and suffering he caused to his victims.

Afterward, Bailey and his former FBI colleague accompanied Pamela Miller's mother to the motel where they stayed.

She broke out a bottle of sparkling wine, popped the cork, and the trio toasted to the memory of her daughter.

A Legacy of Evil

Now-retired Special Agent Tase Bailey says the viciousness and cruelty of the Camacho case continue to haunt him.

The brazen brutality is unthinkable. To illustrate that point, Bailey recalled the equipment rental manager's reaction when FBI agents showed up to seize the tree mulcher for evidence. He thought someone was playing a joke on him.

Bailey says Camacho was just plain evil, and it's the same sinister force we see today in the brutality of the Mexican drug cartels.

The case of Geno Camacho stands as a stark reminder of the capacity for human brutality and the relentless pursuit of justice by FBI agents.

It is a testament to the determination of the brave men and women in law enforcement who fight on our behalf in the age-old conflict of good versus evil.

Robert Riggs

The Postman Cometh With A Package That Went Tick, Tick, Tick

A Quiet Morning Shattered

The autumn morning of September 21, 1995, began like any other in Centerville, Texas. At the local barbershop, conversations buzzed with anticipation about the upcoming Tigers football game. The aroma of smoked meats wafted from Woody's Smokehouse, a beloved pit stop where travelers along Interstate 45 between Dallas and Houston could fuel their vehicles and sample some of Texas's finest beef jerky and barbecue.

The historic Leon County courthouse, an architectural gem built in 1886, stood proudly in the town square, its Renaissance Revival red brick facade a testament to the community's deep roots. Few among the town's 900 residents could have imagined that their peaceful county seat, founded in 1850, was about to become the scene of what could have been one of the deadliest domestic terrorism attacks in Texas history.

The Package

As the morning mail carrier made his appointed rounds, his leather satchel was noticeably heavier than usual. Among his deliveries was an ordinary-looking cardboard box, shipped from Dallas the previous day, addressed to Rebecca Roland at the Leon County Probation Department.

Roland, a clerk whose duties included handling incoming mail, accepted the package without suspicion. It was only when she attempted to extract its contents that the first signs of trouble emerged. Inside the cardboard exterior, a metal box remained stubbornly lodged.

Seeking assistance, Roland turned to her office supervisor. What happened next would set in motion a chain of events that would expose a sinister plot of revenge and domestic terrorism.

Thirty Seconds of Terror

The supervisor's attempts to dislodge the metal container were aggressive. He shook it vigorously and repeatedly struck it against a desk until it finally broke free. Upon lifting the lid, he made a discovery that sent shockwaves through the office.

"Bomb, Bomb!" he shouted, his voice carrying the weight of imminent danger.

Former federal prosecutor Bill Johnston, who would later lead the prosecution of the case, recounts those harrowing moments with chilling detail. "There was a distinct click," Johnston explains. "Within thirty seconds, everyone had evacuated the building, their screams echoing through the halls."

What they had uncovered was a sophisticated double-pipe bomb constructed with heavy-grade pipe and carefully machined end caps. The device employed what bomb technicians call "refrigerator switches" – the exact mechanism that activates a refrigerator's interior light when the door opens. In this case, the switches were designed to complete an electrical circuit when the box's lid was raised, triggering a devastating explosion.

A Miraculous Malfunction

The bomb's failure to detonate left experts puzzled. "Everything about its construction was perfect," Johnston notes. "To this day, we cannot explain why it didn't go off."

The gravity of the situation prompted local law enforcement to summon a U.S. Army bomb disposal unit. Their assessment confirmed everyone's worst fears: they were dealing with a live explosive device of extraordinary power.

The Town Square Becomes a Bomb Bunker

In a scene more reminiscent of a war zone than a small Texas town, the courthouse square was transformed into an impromptu bomb disposal site. A lone soldier, demonstrating remarkable courage, carefully transported the device to the center of the square.

"They surrounded it with thousands of pounds of sandbags," Johnston recalls. "The makeshift bunker they created was a testament to the bomb's lethal potential."

The disposal team's method was decisive and controlled. Using a .50 caliber round, they detonated the device from a safe distance. The resulting explosion produced a fireball approximately four feet in diameter, validating their gravest concerns about its destructive capacity.

The True Target Emerges

As investigators began piecing together the puzzle, a disturbing pattern of domestic abuse and stalking emerged. Rebecca Roland, the package's intended recipient, had recently obtained a protective order against her estranged husband, Loren Bruce Pierson.

The history of violence was well-documented. Pierson had previously assaulted both Roland and her teenage daughter with a crutch. When Roland announced her intention to leave the marriage, Pierson's response was unequivocal: he threatened to kill her.

Seeking safety, Roland and her daughter had relocated to a nearby mobile home. But the move provided little respite from Pierson's campaign of terror. He would regularly appear near their new residence, shouting obscene threats and even firing shots at the trailer.

A Calculated Plan

The bombing attempt revealed a chilling level of premeditation. Pierson had chosen a workday for his attack, knowing Roland would be at her desk in the probation office. The potential for collateral casualties appeared to be of no concern to him.

"His plan was particularly devious," Johnston explains. "He was willing to kill everyone in the office and the adjacent bank – potentially 10 to 15 people – just to ensure Roland wouldn't survive."

The Investigation Begins

Initial evidence was frustratingly circumstantial. The package yielded no fingerprints or other obvious forensic traces. A search warrant executed at Pierson's residence initially appeared to hit a dead end.

"We found no black powder, no pipe, no tools that could have been used to construct a bomb," Johnston remembers. "The place was spotless."

However, Pierson's behavior during the search raised red flags. Before investigators could mention anything about the bombing attempt, he specifically inquired about his wife's welfare.

Digital Clues

A breakthrough came from an unexpected direction: typography. The package's mailing label had been printed in Times New Roman font, a common typeface used in word processing. When investigators examined Pierson's Packard Bell computer and printer, they made a telling discovery.

The Times New Roman font had been deliberately deleted from the system on the day of the bombing attempt. "It was clever," Johnston admits. "He thought by removing the font, he could prove his computer couldn't have produced the label. Instead, the deletion itself became evidence of his guilt."

The Legal Strategy

While the investigation continued, authorities faced a pressing concern: keeping Pierson in custody and Roland safe. The solution came from recently enacted legislation.

"The Violence Against Women Act had just been passed by Congress," Johnston recalls. "We hadn't received any training on it, but I remembered its existence." After consulting with the Justice Department, Johnston confirmed that Pierson's possession of firearms while under a protective order violated the new law.

The case would mark the first prosecution under this provision of VAWA in the United States. During their search, agents had seized a 30/30 Strum Rifle and a Marlin shotgun from Pierson's home, providing grounds for his detention.

The Forensic Breakthrough

As postal inspectors continued their methodical examination of the evidence, they uncovered Roland's palm and fingerprints on cardboard inserts from the package. Roland identified these as materials she had previously seen in their shared home, adding another link in the chain of evidence.

However, the most crucial piece of evidence came from an unexpected source: animal hair found on the package's tape. Initial analysis revealed it was unlike typical cattle hair despite showing similar characteristics.

The Dog That Solved the Case

A second search warrant allowed investigators to vacuum Pierson's house and seize his vacuum cleaner bags. The forensic analysis that followed provided the smoking gun: the hair on the bomb package matched the distinct characteristics of hair from Pierson's large mixed-breed dog.

"It was almost one in a million," Johnston explains. "The clear hairs with ovoid bodies found in his vacuum perfectly matched the single hair found on the bomb package's tape."

Justice Served

The combination of circumstantial evidence, digital forensics, and the damning dog hair proved sufficient for conviction. Despite having no known background in explosives or bomb-making, Pierson had constructed what experts described as a "beautiful bomb." He was sentenced to 38 years in federal prison.

Epilogue

Loren Bruce Pierson died in federal custody in January 2012, having served 16 years of his sentence. He was 62 years old. His death marked the final chapter in a case that highlighted the devastating intersection of domestic violence and terrorism in small-town America.

The case stands as a testament to the evolving nature of forensic science, where evidence as seemingly insignificant as a single dog hair can crack open a case that might otherwise have gone unsolved. It also underscores the importance of domestic violence legislation and the critical role of multi-agency cooperation in bringing dangerous offenders to justice.

For the residents of Centerville, Texas, the events of September 21, 1995, serve as a reminder that even in the most peaceful communities, darkness can lurk behind ordinary facades. The historic courthouse square, once briefly transformed into a battlefield, continues to stand as it has since 1886, bearing silent witness to both the darkness and light of human nature.

The case of the Centerville bomb remains one of the most significant domestic terrorism investigations in Texas history, not just for what happened but for what was prevented: a massacre that would have forever changed the face of this small Texas town.

Robert Riggs

11 Days of Terror: The Deadly Hostage Crisis Behind Texas Prison Walls

Huntsville, Texas, became the center of national attention as a tense prison hostage crisis unfolded inside its first state prison known as the "The Walls Unit." For 11 days behind its 15-foot red brick wall in the sweltering summer of 1974, three armed inmates held fifteen people hostage, culminating in a violent shootout that left two hostages and two inmates dead.

The longest prison siege in American history started at 1 PM on Wednesday, July 24th of 1974, inside the unit's education building. Frederico "Fred" Gomez Carrasco, a 34-year-old notorious drug lord serving a life sentence for the attempted murder of a San Antonio policeman, and two other armed inmates stormed the prison library located on the third floor of its education building.

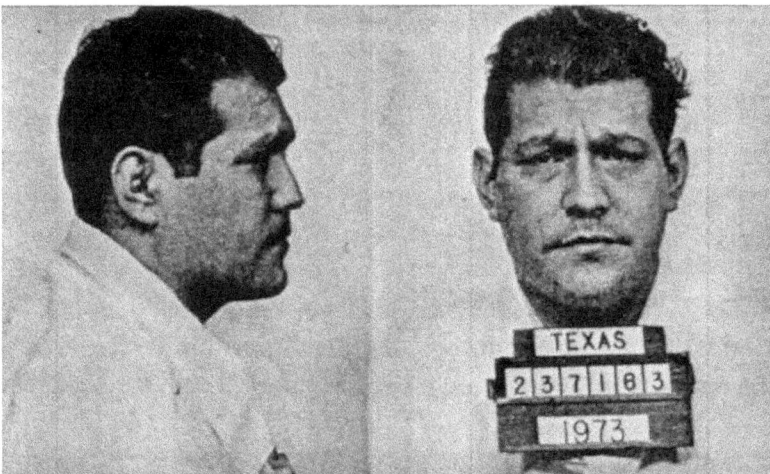

Fred Carrasco, Ringleader of Deadly 1974 Hostage Crisis

Fred Carrasco, infamously dubbed the "Mexican Connection" by law enforcement, was the Pablo Escobar of his time, a notorious drug lord whose empire and ruthless tactics echoed those of the infamous Colombian kingpin. He ruled a vast cocaine and heroin empire spanning from San Diego to Chicago. Born and raised in San Antonio, Texas, Carrasco embarked on his criminal journey at fifteen.

By the late 1960s, he had ascended to the pinnacle of his illicit career. Operating from Nuevo Laredo, Texas, Carrasco maneuvered seamlessly across the United States and Mexico, largely undeterred by authorities.

Carrasco's ruthless reputation was immortalized in Spanish ballads, celebrated in local dance halls, and feared by many. He boasted about gunning down 47 men. His tales of violence and audacity earned him the fearsome moniker "El Señor" (The Man). His legend, marked by gun-slinging bravado and a chilling body count, cemented his status as one of Texas's most feared and deadly figures in the drug trade.

Aiding Carrasco were inmates 42-year-old Ignacio Cuevas, considered by fellow convicts as a real "nut case," and 28-year-old Rudolfo (Rudy) Dominguez, described by the prison chaplain as a "vicious man" who believed in nothing. During the ordeal, the hostages believed Dominguez was the inmate most likely to harm them.

Among the hostages was Ann Flemming, a 50-year-old librarian who had been working at the prison for just 20 days. Just as the prison whistle blew to signal that lunch had ended, Carrasco rose to his feet and fired a single round into the ceiling of the library from a three fifty seven caliber revolver. Carrasco shouted, "Stop right there, or I will kill you!"

Flemming recalled her experience during an interview twenty years ago. "The thing that really amazed me," she said, "was how everyone — men, women, guards — was terrorized. I was afraid. I realized that there was no way out."

Carrasco used an inmate trustee who worked outside the prison during the day to smuggle weapons and ammunition into the formidable red-brick prison that dominates downtown Huntsville. His gang threatened to kill the inmate's family if he failed to cooperate.

They concealed a 38 caliber revolver inside a hollowed-out ham, wrapped two three fifty seven caliber revolvers in packages of meat, and hid hundreds of bullets inside a huge can of peaches. This elaborate smuggling operation occurred before metal detectors became commonplace in prisons, airports, and government buildings.

The prison system would have assigned Carrasco to a maximum-security unit, but he was recovering from three gunshot wounds inflicted by San Antonio police a year earlier. Instead, officials confined him to the medium-security Walls Unit due to its proximity to a prison hospital and lower risk of an escape attempt.

The five foot seven tall, two hundred ten pound dangerous inmate was given light duty as a janitor for Father Joseph O'Brien, the 46 year old prison chaplain. Exploiting this position, Carrasco illicitly used the prison chapel's telephone to make long-distance calls to his gang. When Carrasco seized the library, he revealed hundreds of rounds of ammunition that he had cunningly taped around his legs and concealed under his pants.

Two of the hostage takers opened fire on Lieutenant Wayne Scott and Sergeant Bruce Noviske when the unarmed officers ran up a ramp leading to the prison library. A bullet grazed the shirt worn by Wayne Scott, who is now the former Director of the Texas Department of Criminal Justice, and a Noviske received a flesh wound to his left foot.

After taking over the library, Carrasco barricaded the entrance with a large file cabinet. He forced hostages to take turns sitting on top of it to deter a rescue assault. The only entrance was a double plate glass door that opened to a two story tall winding exit ramp.

To prevent inmates from being distracted during school classes, the prison system had covered the library's windows with bricks, rendering officers unable to see inside or deploy tear gas canisters. As a result, they covertly monitored the situation by slipping a microphone down a pipe chase.

Carrasco took eleven prison employees hostage, consisting of seven women and four men, plus an additional four inmates. Father Joseph O'Brien, who initially acted as a messenger, volunteered to stay with the hostages after the release of one who suffered a heart attack. During the first day, Carrasco released 56 inmates in exchange for a TV and 15 pairs of handcuffs, used later to restrain the hostages.

Later, Carrasco demanded three Army M-16 rifles with full ammunition magazines and 100 rounds for each, three bulletproof vests, helmets, plus walkie-talkies. Carrasco wasn't going any farther than the prison walls. Texas Department of Corrections policy strictly forbade the release of prisoners in exchange for hostages, setting the stage for a prolonged standoff.

The *Huntsville Item* newspaper published its first extra since World War II, knocking President Richard Nixon's Watergate Scandal off its front page.

As news of the siege spread, Huntsville transformed into a media circus. Reporters from across the country descended on the small town, broadcasting live updates and speculating on the fate of the hostages. The crisis became a national spectacle, with millions of Americans following the drama as it unfolded.

Inside the library, the situation was tense and unpredictable. James Estelle Junior, the Director of the Texas Department of Corrections known as the TDC, and officials set up a command post in the warden's office dubbed the "Think Tank." Estelle, assisted at times by Rueben Montemayor, Carrasco's attorney from San Antonio, engaged in marathon negotiations and used stalling tactics. The mercurial psychopath repeatedly threatened to shoot or blow up the hostages if Estelle did not meet his demands. Dominguez and Cuevas tormented the hostages by brandishing guns at their heads.

Carrasco attempted to manipulate the hostages and their families, coercing some into crying during phone calls, including one with Governor Dolph Brisco on the second day of the standoff.

Repeatedly threatened with death, some hostages sharply criticized the Texas Department of Corrections for not yielding to Carrasco's demands, believing it was the only way to secure their release.

In one moment, Carrasco would threaten to kill the hostages if his demands were not met within ten minutes. In the next, he would calm down and request Kentucky Fried Chicken to eat.

During the takeover, Carrasco released four hostages at different intervals, including the prison's director of education, who suffered a heart attack on the first day, and a librarian who faked a heart attack. An inmate hostage, desperate to avoid implication, escaped by diving through a plate glass door on the sixth day. Carrasco freed a final hostage on the tenth day of the standoff to present his escape plan to prison director Estelle.

Meanwhile, Warden Howell Husbands had to maintain order among nineteen hundred inmates. The dining hall was below the library, and the slightest sounds would set off the paranoid hostage takers. Husbands had to lock down the unit and serve sandwiches in paper bags to the cells.

It became clear to Estelle and FBI agent Bob Wiatt that Carrasco did not have a well-thought-out escape plan. At the start of the siege, officers surrounded the prison and Huntsville with a security blanket to thwart any attempt by Carrasco's gang to make his getaway. Rumors circulated that the gang planned to kidnap officer's families.

Carrasco demanded expensive men's apparel to replace their white inmate uniforms, bulletproof vests, helmets, walky-talkies, and weapons. Estelle provided thirteen hundred dollars worth of suits and dress shoes.

Fearing that prison snipers would shoot them in the head, Carrasco ordered the creation of three steel helmets to protect them. The headgear resembled the armor the Knights of King Arthur's Roundtable wore. These helmets are now on display at the Texas Prison Museum in Huntsville.

The hostage takers talked among themselves about escaping to Cuba, where they thought Communist dictator Fidel Castro would give them sanctuary.

On the eighth day of the siege, Carrasco demanded an armored truck. While officials did provide the truck, they gave no assurances that he would be allowed to drive away with the hostages.

The inmates built a makeshift "Trojan Horse" to cover their escape to the waiting armored truck. They taped together a pair of six-by-six-foot chalkboards fortified with 700 pounds of library law books wrapped around the outside as a shield.

At 9:27 pm on the eleventh and final day of the standoff, Carrasco and his two henchmen secured themselves inside the three-foot space between the chalkboards. They handcuffed themselves to three hostages who volunteered to get inside the contraption: teacher Von Beseda; librarian Judy Standley; and prison school principal Novella Pollard. Prison Chaplain Father Joseph O'Brien also got inside.

The conspirators handcuffed the remaining eight hostages, consisting of civilian employees and inmates, to a rope wrapped around the outside of the Trojan Horse. They were supposed to maneuver the rickety shield down a winding ramp.

Civilian & Inmate Hostages Guide Trojan Horse Down Ramp

Prison Director Estelle had no intention of letting Carrasco and his confederates reach the armored truck.

An assault team hid, waiting with a high-pressure fire hose.

When the Trojan Horse jammed against the handrail on the last right-angle turn of the four-turn ramp. Officers yelled for the hostages to duck.

They unleashed torrents of water onto the Trojan Horse. However, the plan to knock over the Trojan Horse went awry when the hose came loose, causing a significant drop in the water pressure.

As soon as the first water blast hit the shield, Carrasco pumped a deadly hollow point round into Von Beseda's heart. Dominguez fired three deadly rounds into Judy Standley's back. Another bullet splintered Father O'Brien's left arm and lodged fragments near his heart. Inmate Cuevas faked passing out and fell, taking Pollard down as bullets zipped above them.

Gunfire erupted from inside the Trojan Horse through gun ports Carrasco and his accomplices had cut in the chalkboards. A twenty-two-minute gun battle ensued. FBI agent Bob Wiatt took two rounds in the chest of his bullet-resistant vest. Texas Ranger Captains James (Pete) Rogers and G.W. Burks also took hits in their vests. The three officers quickly recovered and rejoined the fight.

Officers used a ladder as a battering ram to topple the shield. Amidst the gunfire, TDC Lieutenant Willard Stewart bravely cut the hostages loose from outside the Trojan Horse, saving their lives.

The toppled Trojan Horse exposed Carrasco, who had shot himself in the head. A Department of Public Safety Intelligence officer lunged into the fray and delivered three fatal shots into Dominguez.

Trojan Horse Shield Jerry Rigged Chalkboard
Covered With Library Law Books

Inmate Cuevas, pretending to be unconscious, slid down the ramp in a stream of bloody water and was taken into custody. His hostage, Novella Pollard, escaped unharmed. Prison Chaplain Father Joseph O'Brien survived the gunshot wounds.

The last shots were fired at 9:50 pm, ending the eleven-day siege on the moonlit night of August 3rd of 1974.

Helmets Used By Inmates During The Escape Attempt

Seventeen years later, Ignacio Cuevas was executed by lethal injection inside the death chamber of the Walls Unit, where he had taken part in the murders of Von Beseda and Judy Standley.

The San Antonio police officers who were in the shootout that had sent Carrasco to the Walls Unit later said, "We should have killed him when we had the chance."

The Texas Prison Museum commemorated the historic prison siege on its 50th anniversary during an event in Huntsville called 11 Days in Hell held on July 27th of two thousand twenty-four.

I had the honor of moderating an emotional tribute that united families of the slain hostages and the officers who risked their lives to end the longest prison siege in United States history.

ELIZABETH BESEDA   ANTHONY BRANCH   BERTHA DAVIS   ANN FLEMING

BOBBY HEARD   ALINE HOUSE   GLEN JOHNSON   FATHER JOSEPH O'BRIEN

NOVELLA POLLARD   RONALD ROBINSON   JULIA STANDLEY   LINDA WOODMAN

Hostages Held In 1974 Huntsville Prison Siege

Robert Riggs

www.ingramcontent.com/pod-product-compliance
Lightning Source LLC
Chambersburg PA
CBHW072114270326
41931CB00010B/1559